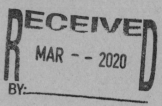

THREE
BROTHERS

YAN LIANKE

THREE BROTHERS

Memories of My Family

Translated from the Chinese by Carlos Rojas

Grove Press
New York

Three Brothers was first published in China in 2009
by Yunnan People's Press as Wo yu fubei.

Published simultaneously in Canada
Printed in the United States of America

First Grove Atlantic hardcover edition: March 2020

This book is set in ITC Berkeley Oldstyle with Adobe Caslon Pro
by Alpha Design and Composition of Pittsfield, NH.

Library of Congress Cataloging-in-Publication data is available for this title.

ISBN 978-0-8021-4808-7
eISBN 978-0-8021-4809-4

Grove Press
an imprint of Grove Atlantic
154 West 14th Street
New York, NY 10011

Distributed by Publishers Group West

groveatlantic.com

20 21 22 23   10 9 8 7 6 5 4 3 2 1

Preface

The Home from
Which I Walked Away

Some people spend their entire lives in their own home, village, or city, while others spend their lives elsewhere. There are also some people who end up constantly traveling back and forth between home and another place.

When I was twenty, I left home to join the army. This was the first time I took a train, the first time I watched television, the first time I heard about Chinese women's volleyball, and the first time I had the chance to eat limitless amounts of dumplings and meat buns. It was also the first time I learned that there were three categories of fiction: short stories, novellas, and novels. It was also back in 1978, while I was living in the military barracks, that I became enthralled by the solemnity and even the smell of China's literary journals, *People's Literature* and *Liberation Army Literature and Arts*. It was around this time that I happened to see, on the cover of a book in the city library, a picture of the blue-eyed Vivien Leigh. I was shocked by her beauty, and for several minutes I stared dumbfounded at the picture. I couldn't believe that foreigners looked like this, that there could be people in this world who appeared so different from us. So I checked out all three volumes of the Chinese edition of Margaret Mitchell's *Gone with the Wind*, each of which had a cover with a picture of Leigh from the film adaptation, and over the course of three nights I finished the entire thing. I had assumed that the rest of the world's fiction was identical to the revolutionary stories and the Red Classics that I had read, and this was how I came to realize how limited and warped my understanding of literature was.

I began excitedly reading works by Western authors such as Tolstoy, Balzac, and Stendhal. While reading Hugo's *Les Misérables*, I felt my palms grow sweaty, thinking that Jean Valjean might step out from the book's pages, a thought that was so disturbing that I frequently had to close the volume and crack my knuckles just to distract myself. Similarly, while reading Flaubert's *Madame Bovary*, I would wake up in the middle of the night and go out to the military drill grounds, and only after running a lap in the frigid cold would I return to my dormitory and continue devouring the novel. But it was Margaret Mitchell who truly transported me to another world, a casually dressed maid leading me into a solemn church.

It was at this time that I began to commit myself to reading and writing, and even submitted manuscripts for publication. In 1979 I published my first short story, which unfortunately is now lost. For that work, I received eight yuan, which made me more excited than an 800,000 yuan payment would today. I used two yuan to buy candy and cigarettes for my company and platoon leaders, as well as my fellow soldiers. Then I pooled the remaining six yuan with the earnings I'd saved up from the preceding three months, leaving me with a total of twenty yuan, which I mailed home to help pay for Father's medicine. Over the next few years I managed to publish one or two stories a year, from which I earned between a dozen and several dozen yuan. I sent almost all of my payments home, and Mother or Elder Sister would give the money to the town pharmacy or hospital for Father's medicine and treatment. Eventually I was promoted to cadre and got married, but I secretly still dreamed that one day I might be able to become an author. If I did, Father would feel that I had truly succeeded in establishing both a career and a family—meaning that he could now depart from this life.

The same way that a tree can bear fruit, and the fruit can decay, die, or yield a new fruit tree, over time, a single household can grow into a village. Everything is merely a repetition or a reenactment of this same basic process of growth. Regardless of whether you spend your entire life on a single plot of land or leave home and seek your fortune elsewhere, it is impossible to escape your destiny.

I never stop to ponder things beyond fate, because accepting fate is my only way of approaching the world. When Father told me to go seek my fortune, I began struggling to achieve that "fortune." When Margaret Mitchell showed me a new world, I began exploring it. I set about reading and writing, establishing my career and earning money, and when I was tired I would return to my family home and chat with my mother and my siblings, and do what I could to help out the other villagers. After recovering my strength I would leave again, only to return when I was tired. I believe that this process of traveling to and from the village is a trajectory arranged for me by heaven.

In 1985, my son was born, and my mother moved from our hometown in the countryside to the old city of Kaifeng, to help with the baby. That also happened to be the same year that I published my first novella in the now-defunct journal *Kunlun*. Running just under forty thousand Chinese characters, the novella earned me almost 800 yuan, and our family was almost more excited to receive this vast sum than we had been by the birth of our son. To celebrate, the entire family went to a restaurant and wolfed down a meal, and we also purchased an eighteen-inch television set. From the 1979 publication of my first short story to the 1985 publication of my first novella, I had endured six years of hardship and toil, and my family understood how this was bittersweet. Mother, however, took that thick copy of *Kunlun* and leafed through the twenty-odd pages containing my story, then remarked, "You were able to earn 800 yuan for such a short piece? This is much better than a peasant farming the land. If this is the deal, then you should spend the rest of your life writing!"

I similarly felt that this line of work was much better than being a peasant. I didn't have to endure adverse weather, and had the opportunity to attain a degree of power and fame. This was definitely something to which I could devote my whole life. When I had left home, Father had exhorted me to go seek my fortune, and Mother was now recommending that I continue writing—so what reason did I have to stop? Later, during the golden age of contemporary Chinese literature, a television series for which I had written the screenplay was broadcast on CCTV at prime time for three years, and royalties for this script were larger than the ones I received for my fiction. I was able to send Mother so much money every month that she felt she wouldn't be able to spend it all even if she ate meat every day. Furthermore, every New Year the town mayor, county mayor, and county party secretary would come to our house to offer us their greetings, and consequently all the other villagers realized I had become famous enough for the county mayor to visit me and invite me out to eat. It was as though a household had, in the blink of an eye, succeeded in becoming not merely a village but an entire city, and during that period our home's appearance and spirit were like the arrival of spring after a bitterly cold winter. Even the calls of the sparrows on the tree branches and the house's eaves sounded different from before.

In 1994 one of my novellas ran into trouble, and consequently I had to spend six months penning self-criticisms. During this period I spent all day writing self-criticisms and all night working on my own fiction, until in the end my lumbago and spinal arthritis began flaring up. Eventually my health deteriorated to the point that I had to write while lying flat on my back in bed. I even needed someone to bring me food and put it right in my hand. During this period, Mother, Elder Brother, and Elder Sister came to the barracks to visit me. When Mother saw that I was unable to walk or even sit up, and instead was lying flat on my back on a stretcher the Federation for Disabled Persons had built specifically for me, with a movable board positioned directly above my head so I could still write, she exclaimed, "Have you driven yourself insane with your writing? Have you taken a perfectly good person, and transformed him into a disabled one?" Elder Brother looked at the stretcher and the frame holding my writing board, and asked, "Why bother with all of this? . . . Isn't living well ultimately more important than these things you want to write?" Meanwhile, my sisters both said the same thing: "We are already living quite comfortably now, so there is no need for you to lie here every day and continue writing these things people don't like."

There was a period of silence, after which my family began urging me to stop writing, adding that if I felt I really had to continue, I should at least focus on things people like—such as screenplays for television series on CCTV. Thinking back, I realize that these were not merely my family's own words, but were the voice and the sentiment of the entire village. At the time, however, I couldn't understand this collective voice and spirit and, instead, nodded as earnestly and piously as if I were writing a self-criticism. After my family left, I continued lying on that stretcher, writing my novel *Streams of Time*. After *Streams of Time*, I wrote the novella *The Years, Months, Days*, as well as the novels *Hard Like Water* and *Lenin's Kisses*. After the publication of *Lenin's Kisses*, however, I was forced to leave the army and find a new employer, following which I wrote two more novels that incited even greater consternation. During that year's Lunar New Year festival, our county's mayor called me up and announced, "Lianke, I want to tell you something undeniably true: you are now our county's most unwelcome resident!"

Upon hearing this, I abruptly realized what kind of transformation my relationship with that region had undergone. It was as though an ox had accidentally trod on the body of the farmer charged with looking after it.

After I learned that I was our region's most unwelcome resident, three days passed without my leaving the house. I didn't find the mayor's remark humorous, nor did I see it as a drunken rambling. Instead, it was an articulation of the region's attitudes and positions, given in the local accent. At this point I began to ponder the relationship between my writing and this land. I noticed that while the land could very easily do without me, I couldn't survive without the land. Without me, the land would just follow its current trajectory. The sun would continue to rise and set, and life would go on as it had for over a thousand years. However, without that land, I would no longer be myself. Without that village, I would be nothing. I reflected that perhaps I had strayed too far from that land, that I had forgotten the color of the soil. I had eaten and drunk my fill from that land, and then had taken enough food and essentials to move forward for a long time without looking back. This is how I ended up straying so far afield, to the point that I almost forgot where I was born and had grown up. Even the relatives still living on that land didn't believe that I still had any close ties there.

I had to return again to that land.

When I came home for the New Year celebration in 2012, I was prepared to ignore the people disparaging, critiquing, and cursing my family. But as it happened that year our family enjoyed an unusually peaceful and congenial holiday period. When I went to visit my relatives, I heard the flowing river, which reminded me of how I would sing exuberantly in the fields when I was a child. Together with my mother, sisters, and sister-in-law, I watched the television series *My Fair Princess* and ate New Year dumplings and stir-fried dishes. That entire visit, until I left home on day five of the new year, I didn't hear a single critique of me or my writing. But, after the festivities had concluded and I was about to depart, Elder Brother smiled bitterly and said, "When you go back, perhaps you could write other sorts of things? You could write something different!" And as I was driving back to Beijing, the nephew escorting me murmured, "Uncle, my grandmother asked me to speak to you on her behalf, and tell you that it is still possible to live a good life without writing. There is no need for you to hang yourself from this tree of writing . . ."

I really was going to hang myself from this tree of writing.

I knew I had strayed too far from the original wishes of my parents, my sisters, my elder brother and his wife, and my fellow villagers. I felt like a child who runs away from home when he is young, and when he approaches sixty and finally decides to return to his hometown and live out his old age, discovers that he can't even find the house where he grew up. In fact, he can't even find the village. I felt like a child who adopts a religion but then rarely encounters a church or mosque, or a Buddhist or Taoist temple, and consequently although he might have God in his heart, over time he might forget what a church or temple is, and when he returns home he might not even recognize these places of worship.

In this case, it is not the church that rejects the believer, but rather the believer who abandons the church.

Some might say that a home to which one cannot return is the only true hometown. My hometown never rejected me, and whenever I return almost everyone welcomes me and appears to be proud of me. However, I don't dare tell them what exactly I spend my days writing. I am this region's unfilial son, an enemy agent, and the reason everyone still smiles when I return is that they don't know that I'm a traitor to their land.

I heard that during the War of Resistance against Japan, in a village in the Northeast there was a traitor who was able to enjoy a good life by selling out his relatives. It was said that every time he went into the city pretending to do business but actually to deliver intelligence reports to the Japanese, he would always return with many small goods that were scarce at that time, and would distribute them to his neighbors and fellow villagers. The neighbors and villagers all viewed this traitor as the most generous person in the village, and even in the entire northeast region. Even after he was executed following the end of the war, none of the locals could believe that he was an unfilial son and a traitor.

I often wonder whether it has been by betraying my land that I have managed to achieve fame and fortune, whether this is how I have managed to live a comfortable life. However, even if I completely abandon my home and my land, our family's front door will still be open, awaiting my return. Whenever I return home, which I do sometimes several times a year, all of my relatives, neighbors, and fellow villagers know that I've come back, but I am the only one who knows that I have not truly returned to the home of my youth. My body may have returned, but my spirit continues to hover over the fields beyond the village. I do not want my family and neighbors to know what I have said, done, or written while I was away—the same way that that traitor from the Northeast did not want those in his village to know what he had said and done in the city. So whenever I return home, I am meek and silent with my mother, siblings, and other relatives. I smile and nod pleasantly and, regardless of what is said, always feign a look of devoted attention. Nevertheless, I know that between me and that piece of land there is a wall I have built and which only I can see.

It might appear that the world and human affairs are static, but in reality things are constantly changing. Not long ago, during the first half of this year, I once again returned home to rest and recover my strength. After dinner, everyone sat around awkwardly, silence pressing down on us like a black haze. Father's funeral portrait was sitting on the table staring at me, while Mother, my sisters, and my brother and his wife all remained silent and stared down at the ground. At that moment—after perhaps a few seconds, though maybe it was a few years or even centuries—Elder Brother began to speak.

He said to me, "Lianke, you're already sixty, right?"

I laughed. "Yes. From the time I left home to join the army, it has already been forty years."

No one could believe it had already been four decades since I left home, just as even I couldn't believe that I was already sixty. Everyone was struck by this reminder of the inexorable passage of time, like someone who is hit on the head by a club but can't believe that the attack has occurred, though the blood seeping out through the cracks in time proves that it is true. Elder Brother then adopted a tone similar to our father's, and said, "You are already sixty, and have read many books. While you are away from home, you should do whatever you want."

Then Mother said, "I'm already eighty-five. While you are away from home, you should write whatever you want, just as long as you return every year to visit me and this home."

And then . . . and then I suddenly felt relaxed. There was silence again, the silence between people who meet again after a long separation. It was as though the physical architecture of a church had recognized a believer who had returned after a long absence, and then used its bricks and tiles, its beams and rafters, as well as the pictures and objects hanging from its walls, to embrace its lost child.

This church would welcome this person to sit in the center of the building, where he could rest, reflect, ponder, and murmur. It would say to him, "If you continue going away, and want to go even further, then this church will follow along behind you. You don't need to worry that you've left the church behind, since regardless of where you go, and regardless of how far you travel, your home and your land will always be under your feet."

Beijing, October 5, 2018

CHAPTER 1

Preliminary Words

In an instant, I finally understood that the function of all the toil and hardship, misfortune and kindness my father's generation experienced had been to permit them to continue living, to help them secure daily necessities, and to prepare them for the inevitable processes of aging, disease, and death.

On October 1, 2007, as our country was celebrating the National Day holiday, with happiness inundating cities and towns like a raging flood, I received several phone calls urging me to return to my hometown as quickly as possible, as my sixty-nine-year-old Fourth Uncle had abruptly left this world. Hurrying back from Beijing to Song county in Henan province, I realized with a shock that of the four men in my father's generation—which included three brothers and a cousin—all three brothers had now departed this world, seeking peace and tranquility in another realm.

In the middle of the following night, I knelt down in front of a white spirit tent, keeping vigil over Fourth Uncle's coffin. Outside, the moon was bright and the stars were sparse. There was only a light breeze and the trees were still. The entire village seemed to have stopped breathing in response to Fourth Uncle's death. In the ensuing stillness, one of my sisters went up to the coffin to replace an incense stick that had burned down. When she returned, she said, with some embarrassment, "Brother Lianke, you've written so many books, why don't you write one about our family?"

She said, "Our father's generation have now all passed away. Why don't you write about the three brothers?"

She said, "You can also write about yourself—about your youth."

I didn't immediately respond. Originally I had felt that my writing was completely unrelated to my family and had no relevance to this corner of the world. But at that moment, I happened to be feeling particularly unhappy, hopeless, and confused about my writing. So I decided I absolutely should write something for them—for my father's generation as well as my siblings and cousins. It didn't matter if I wrote neither a lot nor particularly well, as long as they knew that I had written something. So I began examining the life and fate of my father's generation, revisiting my childhood and youth, and researching the historical traces of that period. Finally, I had an epiphany and realized that the function of all the toil and hardship, misfortune and kindness my father's generation experienced had been to permit them to continue living; to help them secure daily necessities like kindling, rice, oil, and salt; and to prepare them for the inevitable processes of aging, disease, and death. I pondered this for a long time, and ultimately decided to write about how they had lived their lives and how they had confronted death. After careful consideration, I decided that my father's generation lived like dust in the wind, primarily for the sake of daily necessities, while people today live for the sake of obtaining a piece of land. But who can escape the need to secure daily necessities and to confront aging and disease? Daily necessities and aging—for many of us, these are the forces that are responsible for our arrival to and departure from this world.

What else is there for us to escape, other than them?

CHAPTER 2

My Era

1. PRIMARY SCHOOL

Historical eras exist because of memory. Some leave tangible traces like knife marks, while others pass by like rain and clouds, detectable only by a faint scent.

I don't know precisely when I was born or started school. My family was from a poor village in central China, and my parents almost always used the lunar calendar. When they did occasionally mention a date in the Western format, all the other villagers would stare in surprise. In the countryside, time is like a sheet of paper ripped from a Western calendar, and it is only because of certain events that historical time exists at all. These events have identifiable dates, the way the wrinkles on an old person's forehead chronicle the passage of time.

The reason that particular year existed is because that was when Second Sister and I enrolled together in a school in the village temple.

On that year's examinations to advance from first to second grade, I scored sixty-one percent on the verbal section and sixty-two percent on the math section. Sixty percent was sufficient to advance to the next grade, so my scores were just enough to push me over the threshold. However, they were low enough to make me feel embarrassed and uncomfortable, and they made it difficult for me to face my parents and fellow villagers. I suspected that the reason my scores were so low was that my second sister, who was in the same grade, had scored quite well. Her verbal and math scores were both in the eighties. Were it not for Second Sister's high scores, my own wouldn't have appeared so low.

I began to hate Second Sister.

Taking advantage of my position as the youngest sibling, I began saying bad things about Second Sister in front of our parents. I began hiding her things, making her think they were lost, so that she would search frantically for them. Then, when our parents scolded her and she began to cry, I would feign concern and proceed to help her find the items in question.

The year before I began second grade we had an unusually cold winter. In the middle of the first lunar month, Second Sister lost her book bag and searched for it until she was bathed in sweat. Mother almost beat her, whereupon I painstakingly—yet actually very easily—found it for her at the head of her bed. Seeing her book bag in my hands, Second Sister began to suspect me, but she had no proof of wrongdoing. After she and I had quarreled at some length, she ultimately had no choice but to give me ten cents as a reluctant expression of gratitude.

I used those ten cents to go out and buy myself a sesame-seed cake. To this day, when I recall that cake I ate, I'm overwhelmed by the memory of its delicious fragrance.

Regardless of how tasty the sesame-seed cake was, in the end I still needed to go to school. I was worried that in second grade I would be assigned to the same class as Second Sister again, which would put me under additional pressure. So on the first day of class, I was deliberately late to school. I dawdled for a long time outside the schoolhouse, like a boxer who is afraid of his opponent and doesn't dare enter the ring, instead waiting hopefully for something unexpected.

And, in fact, something unexpected did happen.

That morning, the sun was shining brightly on the remaining snow, like a mirror reflecting back the light of an entire world. The teacher and students swept up the snow in the school courtyard and then went into the classroom. At the sound of the class bell, there was a brief period of turmoil, and only then did I finally enter the school grounds. At that moment, there appeared a beautiful female teacher enveloped in an intoxicating fragrance. She walked over and asked me my name, and then took me to another classroom, explaining that I had been transferred to her class. She said that Second Sister and I had been assigned to different classrooms in order to help each of us study harder, and hopefully that way we could both advance to the next grade.

At the time, I didn't know to thank God, nor did I realize that life and fate were so reliant on chance and fortune. I just felt that this teacher, who was able to enter people's hearts, was delicate and tender, like scenery touched by the changing seasons. At the time, my gratitude to the school for my education burst forth, like a vast, clear light in a child's heart, almost to the point that it seemed fake. It was as though all the good fortune I would enjoy in life began that day, and all of my misfortune buried at the same time.

As I now pull back the curtain on that period of my life, the first thing I see is the scene that day.

The teacher led me into the classroom and told me to sit in the middle of the first row. Remarkably, the student with whom I was assigned to share a desk was not a boy, nor was it a rural girl. Instead, my desk-mate was a neatly dressed girl with light skin, as plump as a foreign child. If this had been all that was remarkable about her, everything would have been fine. However, as soon as I sat down she used her pencil to draw a line down the middle of our desk, and in the milky-smooth tone of a city girl, she informed me that neither of us could cross that line, and when we were doing our work we mustn't let our elbows touch.

This was the mid-sixties, and it seemed that my subsequent self-awakening—including my self-respect and my understanding of the relationship between men and women, between the city and the countryside, together with my veneration for revolution—all originated in this period. Although I didn't have to worry about academic pressure from Second Sister that semester, there was another more suffocating source of pressure and excitement. Her surname was Zhang. My meeting this plump city girl, whose parents seemed to have some connection to the revolution and to have been reassigned from Luoyang to the commercial wholesale department in our village, became the first fortuitous occurrence that would shape my destiny. Meeting her was a source of enlightenment and gratitude that to this day I can't forget.

My new desk-mate was an excellent student, and consistently scored in the nineties on our weekly quizzes. The difference between our scores reflected a long-standing gulf between rural and urban life. It demonstrated that the line she drew on our desk was not only legitimate but even eminently reasonable. And not only was it reasonable, it was effective. I'm not sure whether it was on her account that I began studying hard, or whether I did so out of a country boy's sense of self-respect and the pitiable modicum of dignity that the contrast between city and countryside bestows. In any event, I began making a secret effort to improve my grades.

Our teacher was tall and slender, but over time her complexion became increasingly sallow. All the students speculated that she probably had hepatitis, which might be contagious. They said that if you got too close to her, you could catch her disease just by breathing the air she exhaled. They said that they had frequently seen her brewing Chinese medicine in her room and also taking some sort of white pills.

In this teacher's class, the students assigned to sit in the first row would often move to the back of the room to avoid her, but I did not. I actually liked sitting in the first row right under her nose, so that I could look up at her slightly sallow yet still very beautiful melon-shaped face, pay attention as she taught writing and math, and listen as she described what had been fresh and new when she was studying in the teaching college in the city. I never said a word to my desk-mate, nor did I ever cross that border on our desk. However, I liked sitting next to her, and in order to catch up to her academic level and lessen the urban-rural divide that separated us, I not only spent the entire day sitting in front of our sick teacher, but after class I even took my homework to the teacher's room to ask her some questions.

I also saw her taking medicine. They were, indeed, white pills.
She asked me, "Aren't you afraid of being infected?"
I shook my head.

She smiled and patted my head. Many years later, when I saw the Indian film *The Vagabond*, there was a brave youth who was kissed on the cheek by the pretty female lead for his bravery, and after the protagonist traipsed away, he continued nostalgically caressing his cheek for a long time. That scene always reminds me of how, back then, I felt as though I were being blessed by that pretty young teacher, and it was precisely that blessing that helped me improve my studies. On our final exams, my desk-mate scored an average of ninety-four on the verbal and math exams, which was the highest in the class. Meanwhile, I scored a ninety-three, the second highest, higher even than Second Sister's score.

Just a single point's difference between my desk-mate's score and mine.

Studying was not even particularly difficult, and I felt that the one-point difference in our scores was less than the width of the paper people sometimes use for windows in place of glass. I thought that if only I could surpass her and have the highest score in the class, it would be like looking up and gazing toward the east before sunrise. During that year's summer vacation, I was bored and listless, and every day seemed to last forever. I was anxious for school to begin so I could once again sit in front of that teacher, listening to her lessons. I was waiting for a new exam as though it were a happy marriage.

However, when the first day of school finally came, my teacher was no longer my teacher.

She had been transferred away.

I heard she had gotten married and moved to the city. It appeared that her new husband was an illustrious man, a county-level cadre. Fortunately, however, my desk-mate was still there. When school started, she secretly gave me a notebook with a red cover, which became my most treasured souvenir during that time. This gift whetted my aspiration to surpass her on the next exam, and to this end, I studied hard and always finished my homework on time. Regardless of who was appointed to lead the class, I would work diligently, and whenever there was something useful to my studies, I would tirelessly pursue it. When we had a supplementary class to learn Chairman Mao's selected quotations, if the teacher asked the students to read a passage, I would recite it from memory. If the teacher asked the students to recite the passage once from memory, I would recite it three or five times.

Our new teacher was a middle-aged man from the countryside, and he never gave quizzes and exams. At that time, I was anticipating an exam in the way a sprinter hunched over at the start line listens for the sound of the starting gun. I was ready to shoot forward like an arrow and seize the first-place prize that was rightfully mine. My opponent was not Second Sister, nor was it my other classmates. It was my desk-mate. She was plump, clean, light-skinned, and had a foreign affect. She had a soft, sweet voice and spoke in very standard Chinese, not the thick dialect those of us from the countryside spoke, nor did she wear the tattered kind of clothing we wore. She had straight and flawless white teeth and was always neatly and elegantly dressed in the sort of clothes that only people from the city could wear.

However, the two of us were separated by only a single point in our exams.

Just one point.

I spent an entire semester working hard to make up this one-point difference.

Finally, it was the end of the semester.

Finally, it was time for another exam.

Finally, the teacher announced that there would be an exam the next day, that students should bring pen and ink, and that they should be sure to get a good night's sleep beforehand.

I couldn't sleep at all that night. It was as if I were about to take the traditional Chinese civil service exams. An excitement similar to the hazy feeling of being in love, which I had not yet experienced, accompanied me all night, until it was time to go to school. That morning, the sun outside the classroom was large and round, and when it shone in through the window, it illuminated the classroom in such a way that it resembled a brightly lit pond. The images of bodhisattvas painted on the wooden beams of the temple that housed our school reflected onto the classroom's ceiling and walls. I glanced at my desk-mate and noticed that she appeared somewhat nervous, as if concerned that I might beat her.

However, I had no choice. I had no alternative but to attempt to leap across this trench separating the city from the countryside.

I placed my pen on the desk.

I placed my draft paper in the upper left-hand corner of the desk.

Finally, the teacher arrived.

He slowly entered, then walked over and stood next to the lectern. He solemnly gazed at us, at our nervous and excited expressions. Then he smiled wanly and said, "For this year's exams, we will no longer use examination booklets and exercises."

He said, "Chairman Mao told us, 'Our educational policy should ensure that those being educated are able to develop themselves morally, intellectually, and physically, and that they become awakened cultural workers within the socialist system.'"

He said, "So that everyone can become awakened cultural workers within the socialist system, we will no longer use exercises and examination booklets."

He said, "For our exams this year, every student will come up to the lectern and recite several Chairman Mao quotes. Whoever can recite five quotes will advance to the third grade."

When the teacher finished, the students all stared at him.

Then there was thunderous applause.

However, I didn't applaud. Instead, I stared at the teacher in confusion, while glancing at my desk-mate. Initially, she also applauded with the other students, but when she saw that I wasn't clapping, she abruptly stopped.

From that point on, our advancement to the next grade was based solely on our ability to recite Chairman Mao quotes, and I never again had a chance to surpass the girl from the city. To advance to third grade, all I had to do was recite five of Chairman Mao's quotes, and to advance to fourth grade, I would probably need to recite ten or fifteen. In between, there were two years when nobody advanced, because all middle schools, high schools, and colleges were shut down during the Cultural Revolution. During that period, however, I continued attending elementary school, where I studied language, practiced math, and memorized Chairman Mao's quotes and poems, as well as his classic essays, "Serve the People," "In Memory of Norman Bethune," and "The Foolish Old Man Who Moved Mountains."

When I look back at that period today, I'm filled with both joy and a happy sorrow. This is because we didn't have any pressure to study, nor did we have heavy school bags, homework, or parents anxious over their child's failure to advance. During my childhood, apart from playing marbles, happy events included receiving the latest political directives, and watching adults stroll down the street, as well as personally accompanying the school's troops as they marched into villages to celebrate. Even today, the memory of that happiness remains strong.

As for the rest, there was only endless hunger and loneliness and going down to the countryside to cut grass, feed pigs, and take cattle out to graze. This made me feel that the countryside was boring and exhausting, and that the land was dull and monotonous—and this feeling seemed to constrict my heart like a vine. Until I graduated from elementary school, the pretty girls from urban families who had been assigned to the countryside remained in my class. Their presence constantly reminded me of my sense of inferiority and of the gap between city and countryside. This gulf was the origin of my perpetual desire to leave the land—but it would also be a chasm that I would never succeed in crossing.

2. *DREAM OF THE RED CHAMBER*

At long last, we entered the 1970s.

Like many of my classmates, I was promoted to middle school after successfully memorizing *Chairman Mao's Selected Quotations*, *Mao Zedong's Poetry*, and his three classic essays. During my tenure in middle school, however, the form of revolution underwent a fervent transformation. The return of the great political figure Deng Xiaoping meant that our school once again returned to a standard examination system. Just as spring inevitably brings rain, to advance to the next grade there were inevitably exams. But when the time came to take them, for some reason I was no longer driven to make up that one-point gap separating my desk-mate and me. Instead, I was fascinated with reading all the revolutionary novels I could find, including works such as *The Golden Road*, *Revolutionary Tales in an Ancient City*, *Song of Youth*, *Steel Meets Fire*, *Tracks in the Snowy Forest*, and *Bright, Sunny Skies*. At the time, I didn't know that these novels were classified as "Red Classics" and instead assumed that—whether in China or outside—these were the only novels that existed. It was as if horses and cattle didn't know that feed is better than grass and milk is better than water, and instead assumed that ordinary grass and straw and water are the tastiest things in the world. I didn't know that, apart from these novels, there were also works by authors such as Lu Xun, Guo Moruo, Mao Dun, and Ba Jin, as well as Lao She and Cao Yu, together with foreign works and Chinese classics such as Cao Xueqin's *Dream of the Red Chamber*.

In fact, I wasn't even sure whether Cao Xueqin was a man or a woman.

For me, the relationship between the countryside and the city was that the city was the countryside's heartfelt yearning, while the countryside was the city's entrails and its source of nutrition. During that period, our hometown was in the center of a market region several dozen *li* in diameter. On market days, people from the countryside came to our village, Tianhu, while people from our village would go to market in the county seat, thirty *li* away. Meanwhile, people from the city would travel to shop in the ancient capital of Luoyang, a hundred *li* away. I was content with my good fortune that my parents had given birth to me in Tianhu, which was much better than being from an even more remote mountain area. The novels I could read in the village would have been much harder to find if I were somewhere more isolated. I had two elder sisters and an elder brother, and although we faced constant poverty, we were also blessed with boundless prosperity and grace. Father's diligence and endurance set a good model for his children, while Mother's frugality and virtue, combined with her industriousness, ensured that my siblings and I would appreciate life's hardships and beauty. This background became an enormous asset for me and provided an endless emotional reservoir once I started to write.

During our childhood, Eldest Sister was not in good health. In modern medical language, we would say she probably suffered from aseptic vertebral osteonecrosis, and although the condition didn't generate any visible symptoms, it was nevertheless extraordinarily painful. Because of this, she had to withdraw from school and spent most of her time in bed. In order to pass the time, she read the sorts of novels that you could find in rural areas. In fact, she read all the printed material you could find in the countryside at that time. Whatever she read, I also read, and whatever books she had, I would have as well.

I'm filled with gratitude to Elder Sister when I think of how the head of her bed became my first library, thanks only to her illness.

That kind of incomparable sibling affection brings tears to my eyes. To many, this may appear somewhat unreasonable, but it is true. Because of my love of literature, and the way this early revolutionary literature was able to fill the gaps in my youthful soul, I was able to get over the feelings of inferiority from the so-called urban-rural divide separating me from my classmates in speech, appearance, and social status.

I became more open-minded, and when my scores on middle school quizzes were not particularly high, this helped reassure me. Reading novels also helped me all but forget my regret at not being able to make up the gap that separated my scores from those of my desk-mate. Meanwhile, I found many of the stories in those revolution-ary novels absolutely unforgettable and unspeakably sorrowful. In the first or second grade of middle school, I finally heard about the great Chinese novel *Dream of the Red Chamber*, also known as *Story of the Stone*. This and the novels *Romance of Three Kingdoms*, *Water Margin*, and *Journey to the West* were collectively referred to as the four great Chinese masterworks. *Dream of the Red Chamber* was the crown jewel, and while I had already read the other three works since Eldest Sister had copies at the head of her bed, for some reason *Dream of the Red Chamber* was never there. I asked some people in the village who wrote poetry couplets, "Does your family have a copy of *Dream of the Red Chamber*?" These local literati looked at me with surprise, as though my question reflected some secret adolescent desire. However, their reaction served only to further whet my determination to read the novel. One day a boy in my class surnamed Jin, whose elder brother was an air force pilot, told me that because Chairman Mao liked *Dream of the Red Chamber*, other people had trouble finding copies. He said that only cadres who were at least at the level of county chief or army commander were given a copy.

I only half-believed this explanation.

My classmate said his brother had sent him a letter saying that a high-level cadre had given him a copy of the novel, and that as soon as he finished reading it, he would mail it to my classmate, whereupon my classmate would lend it to me.

I was surprised by this and became very worried that the package might get lost in the mail.

Yet by the following semester I had forgotten about the whole thing. One day, however, the classmate removed from his book bag a mysterious package wrapped in several layers of paper, then pulled me aside and thrust it into my hands. I wanted to open it immediately, but when I started to do so he turned pale. So I hid the package in my book bag, and when no one was around, I slipped into the bathroom and opened this mysterious package. It was a book. On the light-colored front cover there was the boldly printed title, *Dream of the Red Chamber*. Printed on the back cover was the line, "For internal distribution only." For some reason, I was overjoyed to see this, but I also trembled with fear. Covered in sweat and with shaking hands, I quickly wrapped up the book and stuffed it back into my book bag.

In class that afternoon, I wasn't able to process anything the teacher was saying. Instead, my mind was on that copy of *Dream of the Red Chamber*, as though it were my favorite lover.

That summer vacation, to earn some money to help treat Eldest Sister's illness, Second Sister and I would get up when it was still dark and proceed to a mountain gully several dozen *li* away, then use a cart to haul stones from the gully to a cement factory in our village. We would sell the egg-size rocks to contract teams doing roadwork, and we would sell larger stones to the commercial departments that were building houses on the roadside. We would work throughout the day without rest, until each of us was breathing heavily and drenched in sweat, as exhausted as sick horses. When I read that copy of *Dream of the Red Chamber* each night, however, I would become utterly engrossed. Tears would stream down my face, and I would sigh deeply as I read the sections describing Daiyu burying flowers, Daiyu's death, and Baoyu's decision to become a monk.

I became so engrossed in my reading that I completely forgot about my schoolwork.

It was also that year, as I was being promoted from middle school to high school, that I once again found my fate determined by my test scores. During that period, because I was so absorbed in literature, I became somewhat confused about real life. My fate, like that of my parents, was to work the land, so I would have no choice but to head out at dawn and work till dusk. I didn't believe that if you were able to get into high school, it might be possible for you to stop working the land and instead become a city resident. Therefore I became reconciled to my situation, thinking there was no way for me to advance. I attended that year's exams the same way that I would go with my classmates to watch an opera performance. At the time, the regulations for advancement specified that all the students with an urban residency permit would be automatically promoted, while those with rural residency permits would be promoted based on their test scores, plus letters of recommendation from their school and their production team. If you considered only test scores, Second Sister's were significantly higher than mine, but if you also took recommendations into account, she would probably fall back behind me, meaning that I would likely be the only one from our family who would advance to high school.

It was around lunchtime that Father brought home the news. It was summer, and the cicada cries were resonating through the tree branches. Father sat in our courtyard, and after explaining to Second Sister and me that only one of us could advance to high school, he just sat there, gazing at us uncomfortably. After a hesitation, he added, "Both of you understand our family's situation, in that we have many mouths to feed, and we also have to care for your elder sister. We really need for one of you to stay behind to work the land and earn some work points."

When Father finished, Second Sister and I stood in front of him holding our rice bowls, neither of us saying a word. There was a pause, as time itself ground to a halt and seemed as if it would never start flowing again. Fate froze between us, as clear water becomes bright ice, and it was as though time had become a block of ice pressing down on our family's courtyard. We remained frozen like this for a long time, a long, long time, until finally Mother emerged from the kitchen with a bowl of rice and said, "Come eat! You can continue discussing this after you've eaten."

We each went to eat our food.

I can't remember whether Second Sister carried her bowl inside or took it somewhere else. As for me, I took my bowl of boiled sweet potato noodles and unrefined black rice and went to sit under a tree. There was no one else under that tree, and as I sat all alone, I found that I simply couldn't summon the energy to eat that bowl of food. It was at that moment—as I was facing a crucial crossroads in my life and confronting the question of whether or not I would continue in school—that an educated youth arrived in our village, sent down from the city. He wore a blue uniform and had his hair parted on one side. He was tall, and as he strolled over from the village street, he nodded to the people he knew. The villagers spoke to him in a respectful tone, and he nodded lazily in return.

Then he walked away.

As for me, I sat there for a long time after he left, gazing at his departing shadow, as though looking at a road leading into the distance. At that moment, I realized that I wanted to continue my studies. I wanted to go to high school. I wanted to seize from Second

Sister the slot she was probably counting on. So, I quickly ate my food and returned home, where I saw that Second Sister had reemerged to get more rice from the kitchen.

We gazed at each other as though we were complete strangers.

That afternoon, I went down to the fields to work, but for some reason Second Sister didn't go.

That night, Second Sister wasn't home for dinner.

After dinner, Second Sister still hadn't returned home.

I asked Mother, "Where is Second Sister?"

Mother replied, "She went to see her classmate."

I shifted questions of fate to the back of my mind, as though temporarily covering a wound with a piece of medicinal plaster. I went to sleep. The moon set, and the stars faded, and in the dim night light outside the window there was half-translucent fog and the sound of crickets. Eventually, in the middle of the night—just as I was about to fall asleep, or perhaps after I had already fallen asleep—I was suddenly aware of the sound of our front door opening. I heard Second Sister's soft footsteps out in the courtyard; they grew heavy as they approached my bedroom door. After a pause, Second Sister pushed open the door and approached my bed.

I sat up.

Second Sister said, "You haven't gone to sleep?"

I grunted in response.

Second Sister said, "Lianke, as for high school, your sister has decided she won't go. You should go."

Upon saying this, Second Sister gazed at me in the moonlight. I don't know whether she could see my expression, but I could vaguely make out her bleak smile. As she turned to leave, she said, "You should study well. Your sister is a girl, so she should stay home to work the land."

After that, there was a long wait for high school to begin. The day before school started, Second Sister bought me a fountain pen, and as she was giving it to me, she had tears in her eyes. Nevertheless, she forced a smile and said, "Study well. You need to make good on your sister's slot as well as your own."

When I tell my son this story now, thirty years later, he stares at me in disbelief. It's not that he can't believe that Second Sister, because she was a girl, decided to let her brother continue his studies in her place, but rather that he can't fathom that there was a long period under orthodox socialism when the nation's rural children were perpetually poor and hungry. Parents at that time were unable to guarantee that their children had enough food to eat, much less that they were able to finish middle school and high school. Rural parents and their children felt as though they had been forgotten by society, and when we remember this period today, we are able to recall only its basic meaning.

3. EXECUTION

My most enduring memory from the seventies is not of revolution but rather of hunger and endless work.

Eldest Sister was sick and spent most of her time in bed. Taking care of her became our family's primary focus. At the beginning of the Cultural Revolution, in 1966, Eldest Sister tried to go to Zhengzhou with her classmates as part of a Red Guard contingent, but she missed home and then couldn't secure a place on the train into the city, so she had no choice but to return, missing her chance to see Chairman Mao.

Although Chairman Mao was a great man, he wasn't a doctor, nor could he help cure Eldest Sister's illness. This reality distanced our family from the revolution, the same way that the countryside is distanced from the city, peasants are distanced from city dwellers, and the poor are distanced from the rich. However, the scent of revolution—like summer heat or winter chill—would seep into our family's house and courtyard and into the village's fields. I remember how in the early seventies, after the peak of the Cultural Revolution's struggle had already passed, the other commune members and I would divide our time between pursuing revolution and promoting production.

One day when I was out in the fields turning over sweet potato seedlings, two trucks full of revolutionary youths carrying machine guns suddenly drove by, whereupon the youths turned to us and fired a round of bullets. The bullets struck the grass at the head of the field, and as the grass trembled and dirt flew through the air, one of my companions, who had previously served in the army, shouted, "Get down!" The commune members all followed his lead and dove into the furrows of the sweet potato field. By the time we got up again, the truck had already disappeared into the distance, carrying away the revolutionaries and their laughter. I don't know where this revolutionary contingent came from or where it went, but at that point our production team began shouting and cursing to the departing truck, "Fuck your grandmother! We're working the land and you're pursuing revolution, so mind your own business! What have we ever done to you?!"

The countryside wasn't the main actor of that era or of the revolution itself. As in today's post–Reform and Opening Up era, during the Cultural Revolution primary emphasis was placed on the city and not on the billion peasants living in the countryside. Historically, China's major actors have always been those who have either participated in or had a close relationship with the revolution. The countryside had been the primary battleground of the revolution during its early years, but after Liberation—apart from the Great Leap Forward and the "Three Years of Natural Disasters"—there had been a fundamental change in the revolution's cast. Now, the masses instead played a supporting role for the political leaders. They became part of the revolution's radiation zone, sacrificial figures for the revolution's ultimate success. The most important lesson from the Great Leap Forward and the Three Years of Natural Disasters is that the revolution does not produce grain, only political fervor. During the Three Years of Natural Disasters, millions of people starved to death, which demonstrated that regardless of the revolution, it was still necessary to work the land.

In order to work the land, you needed students like me, who did their schoolwork but could also cut the grass and take the cattle out to graze. It was hard to say which of these was my primary responsibility and which was secondary. While cutting grass and taking cattle out to graze, I watched my parents work from dawn till dusk and in return receive only endless hunger. This nourished my muddled desire to leave the countryside. It was that year, as I was caught in this moment of confusion, that a large contingent of educated youths arrived in our village.

I didn't know where exactly these educated youths were from, but was sure that they came from the city—either Luoyang or Zheng-zhou. In fact, it turned out that six or seven of them were from Zhengzhou, and one was from Luoyang. The villagers graciously hosted these educated youths in a production brigade office that had been set up specifically for this purpose. The villagers treated them respectfully, as they would their elders, because these educated youths could bring items from the city that were otherwise unavailable in the countryside, such as fertilizer, cloth, and matches. Extreme revolution and the planned economy had led to great material deprivation, to the point that even peasants working the land needed a grain coupon to buy a sesame-seed cake on the street. However, what these peasants received from the government were mostly new work assignments;

they received very few grain coupons, coal coupons, cloth coupons, or other types of government-issued coupons. Although the educated youths didn't have an abundant supply of these sorts of things, what they did have always seemed miraculous. So when they came to the countryside and brought the peasants some things that they urgently needed, the peasants were naturally very grateful and as a result wouldn't let the educated youths go down to the fields and work the land. At most, the peasants would ask the educated youths to stand in front of the fields and watch the crops, blowing flutes and waving their hands to frighten away the birds and the pigs and the sheep that somehow made their way into the fields.

At the time, I was still young, and when I saw how the educated youths from the city didn't have to go down to the fields, how they dressed in clean clothing and spent the whole day strolling around, I came to view them as elite deities, a far cry from us lowly peasants. I didn't hate the educated youths for having been born in the city—I just felt a sense of hopeless resentment over the fact that I had been born in the countryside. When the educated youths played their flutes and strolled in front of the fields, they pointed at the peasants walking past and mocked them. When it was time to eat lunch or dinner, only families considered hygienic in the village prepared food for the educated youths—the popular term for this was "arranged meals." Each family was assigned one or two educated youths, and normally they would have to cook for them for a week, and after a week the youths would switch to another family. My mother valued cleanliness, and every day, after sweeping the entire house, she would also sweep the area around the house. Therefore, ours was considered the most appropriate family to prepare arranged meals for the educated youths.

With this responsibility, Mother and Eldest Sister, whose illness at that point had improved somewhat, had to work for almost an whole day making wheat flour and preparing for the educated youths to come to our house to eat. Ordinarily our family had occasion to eat foods made from refined flour and rice only on New Year's and other special holidays. At all other times, we always used coarse grain, like yellow corn flour or sweet potato flour. Apart from New Year's, the only other time we could enjoy refined grain and rice was during the street markets on the fifth, tenth, and fifteenth days of the new year, when Grandfather would come from an even more remote area to the village to go to the market, and Mother would cook him a bowl of white noodle soup or bake him a white flour bun. When Father was exhausted from working in the field, Mother would occasionally prepare him a special dish using refined white flour. Sometimes, when Eldest Sister's illness was particularly severe, Mother would use white flour to prepare her a bowl of noodles with chopped scallions.

But when it was our family's turn to prepare arranged meals for the educated youths, Mother always had to use white flour. For lunch, she would usually make hand-rolled noodles, and for dinner she would cook oil-fried scallion buns. When the students ate, I would stand nearby with my mouth watering, eagerly awaiting the day I could eat like them. Mother felt it wasn't good for me to stand there watching them, so she would always shoo me away, telling me to go do something else. After a while, so as to not jealously watch the educated youths, I would deliberately avoid them whenever they arrived at our house, and instead I would rush out the door and sit under a tree or on a pile of stones that our neighbors had collected in preparation for building a house. From there I would stare at our front door. I would sit there for ages, entertaining the immature thoughts of a country boy, until finally the educated youths would finish their meal and leave, wiping their mouths with their handkerchiefs as they sauntered back to the village. Only then would I rush home.

Every time I returned, I always hoped the educated youths might have left behind some uneaten food. But each time I would find that they hadn't left anything at all. I was deeply disappointed by this, and I am not sure whether it was that Mother fixed them too little food or just that they were young and still growing (but then again, so was I) and so would always finish whatever they were given.

The youths didn't eat for free. For every meal we would be compensated twenty cents and two grain coupons, which would be left on our table or on the stone bench by our front door each week. In retrospect, I realize that this compensation was far less than the value of what the youths ate. And yet every time they delivered the weekly compensation, Mother would always try to demur, insisting that they were leaving too much. Mother's magnanimity truly made me believe that the money and grain coupons the educated youths gave us must have been worth quite a lot. Perhaps that was why Mother was always so enthusiastic about them coming to eat? Perhaps that was why our family permitted them to enjoy the sort of generous treatment that our own family could taste only on rare occasions? It was only later that several families who had been assigned to prepare these arranged meals went to talk to the village cadres, asking how this practice of preparing meals from refined rice and flour could possibly be sustainable. They said that one or two meals for a month or two was doable but asked, Who could afford to keep this up for six months or an entire year? These families continued preparing arranged meals for the educated youths even as they told the cadres about their own food shortages. Half a year later, the educated youths finally began cooking for themselves, and the villagers gave a sigh of relief, feeling that a heavy burden had been lifted from their shoulders.

In the early eighties there emerged a genre of "educated youth" literature, which presented the countryside as a prison and traced all the authors' suffering back to some ignorant conflicts with the locals over land. This often made me feel that the peasants' inability to truly understand the city and its educated youths represented a disaster for the entire nation. At the same time, however, I am convinced that an even greater catastrophe was the fundamental inability of the educated youths—including those former educated youths who subsequently became authors, poets, and teachers—to truly understand the rural land on which they stayed for years, much less the people who had been living on that land for centuries. Actually, in the remote piece of land where my home was located, there were not nearly as many educated youths as there were in the Heilongjiang construction corps—which employed vast crowds of educated youths, continually moving them in and out of the countryside. But in every village, we nevertheless had a steady stream of educated youths. They resembled tourists but would stay for a period ranging from a few months to a few years.

It was a glorious moment when they finally returned to the city.

I never witnessed or heard of incidents of educated youths in my hometown area experiencing "hardship." However, I knew that for them those memories had already become a form of collective hardship and would become a valuable and happy historical memory. Later, there would be incidents in the village in which chickens, dogs, or even goats or sheep would suddenly go missing, but after looking for days, we'd finally find the dog head or sheep pelt near where the educated youths were staying—hanging proudly, like a flag on display for the enemy to see. This was clearly a case of the city putting on a show for the countryside. To the best of my recollection, we didn't feel a sense of love or hate for the educated youths, nor pride or shame, and even less did we approach them with any enthusiasm or so-called resignation. Instead, we simply felt that their presence was an inevitable component of that era, like a storm that would come and go as forecasted. What is relatively fresh in my memory, and what I recall with considerable discomfort, is that around the year 1975 the authorities executed several criminals on the village's riverbank. One of those executed was a village man, and his death was related to the educated youths. It was said that he climbed the wall surrounding the educated youths' compound in an attempt to rape one of the women. Although he didn't succeed, this was nevertheless considered a very serious crime, and therefore the villager was sentenced to death.

On the day of the execution, there were vast crowds, like those at a temple fair. First the authorities conducted a procession through nearby villages, whereby the criminals, their hands bound, were made to stand on either side of a truck, wearing a placard with their name and crime hanging from their chest. The young peasant who had tried to rape the educated youth was forced to wear a placard with his name in black ink covered by a red X, beneath which was the word *rapist*. On his back, like a criminal condemned to death in a play, he had a second wooden placard with his name and crime.

There were vast crowds watching as the procession truck slowly made its way through the streets.

The people in the crowds took rocks and dried mud and threw them at the alleged rapist. However, they didn't throw anything at the murderer or the arsonist, both of whom had also been sentenced to death.

Then the authorities executed the three prisoners by firing squad.

After several gunshots, everything became silent once again, like the calm after a storm.

After the tide of people receded from the riverbank, I went with some companions to the execution grounds to take a look. We saw that there were patches of blood on the sandy ground, like viscous muddy water that had contaminated the white sand. I was somewhat disappointed. This scene engendered nothing of the fear and respect that I normally felt for the educated youths. Prior to this, there had been a similar incident in an educated youth settlement in an adjacent village, only the roles were reversed. In that case, it was an educated youth who raped a village girl. The girl was sixteen years old and had gone out into the fields to cut grass, whereupon the educated youth tricked her into going into a room, where he raped her. The girl ran crying out of the settlement, then jumped into a river and drowned herself. When the assailant heard that the girl had died, he fled the village in the middle of the night and returned to the city. The girl's parents were inconsolable, and after burying their daughter they petitioned the government for some form of redress. But the local government didn't go into the city to try to seize the perpetrator.

Much less did the government sentence him.

The educated youth committed a rape, and the village girl died. Normally a case involving a death is given highest priority, but in the case of this educated youth, nothing was done. Some government cadres accompanied the youth's parents from the city to the countryside, where they offered the girl's family some monetary compensation as well as the world's most sincere apology. But half a year later, there was this similar incident, in which the perpetrator was a peasant, and although he hadn't succeeded in raping his victim, he was sentenced to death.

In the evening of that day, summer heat and moist air circulated up and down the riverbank. We half-grown children stood on a now-empty section of the riverbank where large crowds had assembled to watch the execution. In that empty expanse, I began to have some more complicated doubts about this world. I no longer held any reverence or envy for those educated youths, and instead was developing a deep-rooted sense of resentment. From that point on I remembered that while in the village, the educated youths had reaped a harvest without working for it and they had enjoyed themselves as though on vacation. I couldn't understand why the revolution and the great people had chosen to send these city children to our village—lacking in both land and grain—where these youths would serve merely as a scourge on us peasants. I eagerly looked forward to their departure, to when they would return home, restoring the peaceful distance between city and countryside.

And then, on a day when I least expected it, they left.

During that summer break I went to Luoyang to join a construction team under Fourth Uncle's direction, doing piecework. Nowadays, people who come from the countryside to find work in the cities are known as migrant workers, but at that time they were just called piecework laborers, and as a piecework laborer I transported bricks and ashes, earning some money to supplement my family's income. At the end of the summer, I returned to the village and heard that the educated youths had departed. It was like hearing that the wind had blown away the clouds. I wasn't in the least surprised to hear that they had left, but that night I found myself thinking about how the village had once again become very peaceful after their departure, and I almost missed the way some drama was always unfolding when they were here.

That night, I remembered a female educated youth, who was surnamed Huang, and that when she was eating arranged meals at our house, Mother would always cut her oil-fried scallion bun into four pieces. Huang was the only educated youth who didn't finish her bun.

Instead, she would take one half and leave the other.

One time when she came to eat, I waited, as usual, on that stone pile outside the house until she left. But after a little while, she emerged from our house, looked around, and then headed straight toward me. Without saying a word, she handed me a bundle wrapped in paper. It turned out she had eaten only a quarter of the bun and was giving me the remainder. After the educated youths departed, I often thought about her and that quarter of an oil-fried bun.

When I went down to work in the fields the day after I had returned from my summer in Luoyang, I took the opportunity to go to some of the rooms in the educated youth settlement. I was thinking I might be able to find something there but instead found the rooms completely bare, as though a storm had just swept through and blown everything away.

4. WRITING

To this day, I don't agree with people who contend that educated youths brought civilization to the countryside or that their arrival enabled the countryside to experience urban civilization and culture. My most distinct impression was that their arrival confirmed that the gap between urban and rural life was far greater than people had thought. The people from the countryside did indeed have an ordinary yearning for and envy of city life, but the educated youths' arrival confirmed that city people show a congenital disdain for peasants and the countryside.

It turns out that among the Four Modernizations described in textbooks, the rural modernization was merely a dream, like something out of the Arabian Nights. After the departure of the educated youths, I came to dimly understand that waiting on the land for some sort of change of fate was not nearly as effective as doing everything in my power to escape the land and attempt to change my fate. It was during my early school days—perhaps when I met my deskmate from Luoyang in second grade—that I first began to cultivate a desire to escape the land. But it was only the arrival of the educated youths that caused that seed to germinate and swell.

I began to yearn for the day when I could enter the city. Like a thief anxious to escape, I spent every day searching for opportunities. One day I borrowed a novel from the head of Eldest Sister's bed. The work, by Zhang Kangkang, was titled *Boundary Line*. Today, more than thirty years later, I no longer recall the novel's plot or any relevant details. However, I do remember that the biography of the author printed on the back cover mentioned that Zhang Kangkang was an educated youth who had gone from the Hangzhou countryside to the Great Northern Wilderness, and as a result of having written this novel and having gone to the Harbin Publishing House to undertake revisions, Zhang Kangkang had been able to remain in the provincial capital of Harbin after the novel was published.

This biographical summary gave me a shock, as I realized that by writing a novel it could be possible to escape the land and move to the city for good. It was also at that time, around 1975, that I had developed a desire to write. It was crazy and ambitious, but I sowed the seed of wanting to write a novel so that I could go to the city to publish it and then move there.

It was at that point that I began secretly writing.

After writing the beginning of a revolutionary novel titled *Mountain of Blood and Fire*, I started high school several kilometers away in the historical hometown of the Song dynasty Neo-Confucian thinkers Cheng Hao and Cheng Yi. Shortly after I joined the high school class, someone gestured toward our language teacher, whose surname was Ren, and told me that Ren not only had attended college but furthermore was writing a novel that would be even greater than *Dream of the Red Chamber*. While *Dream of the Red Chamber* consisted of only four volumes, this teacher's novel would consist of five.

I was suddenly filled with respect for this teacher.

One day in class when the teacher asked me a question, I didn't answer directly but rather turned the tables and asked him, "Are you really writing a novel that will be even longer than *Dream of the Red Chamber*?" The teacher didn't answer, and instead he removed a cigarette packet from his pocket and, right then and there, proceeded to rip off a strip of paper, roll a "gun barrel" cigarette, light it, and audaciously smoke it in front of us. With a mysterious smile, he said, "Have you all read *Dream of the Red Chamber*? If you have a chance, you definitely should." At that point, I didn't realize that *Dream of the Red Chamber* was greater than *Boundary Line*, or that Cao Xueqin was more extraordinary than either Zhang Kangkang or my teacher. But it was Zhang Kangkang and her novel that made me realize that this so-called writing was not particularly mysterious nor was it necessarily something distant and unattainable.

5. A LONELY LIGHT

So I began to write and furthermore resolved to do so every day.

During the day I would go to school, and at night I would lie in bed, tossing and turning as I planned out my story. On Sundays I would go to work in the fields, and at night I would light an oil lamp, place it on the old, damaged chest of drawers next to my bed, and work on my novel about class struggle. I would write about landlords, rich peasants, and poor peasants, as well as exploitation and the exploited, resistance and the resisted, and about how the protagonist, after leaving the countryside, goes to search for the Communist Party.

Writing became my secret life, and it made me feel that my youth was more substantial and idealistic than that of my classmates or the other villagers. It was as if I now had a brighter future hanging in the distance, and this made me feel that, thanks to literature, my life now had meaning and that my writing thereby had a yesterday, a today, and—perhaps—a bleak and difficult tomorrow.

Today my works, whether good or bad, total more than five million characters, and when reporters interview me, invariably they ask which author and which work have had the greatest influence on me. I always sincerely answer that the author who had the greatest influence on me was actually Zhang Kangkang and the literary work that most affected me was *Boundary Line*.

I have to admit that I truly feel an inexpressible feeling of gratitude for my "elder sister" Zhang Kangkang.

Time is like a stack of useful or useless writing paper, and days are like useful or useless writing. I turned over page after page, as though writing a meaningless novel. Finally, I had written more than three hundred pages of my first novel when I withdrew from high school, having finished only one semester of the second year. Eldest Sister's back pain was getting progressively worse and our family, in order to purchase daily necessities such as oil, salt, and medicine, needed someone to go to work and earn more. I wasn't yet seventeen years old, but after spending a few days at home packing up my bedding, clothing, and manuscript, I went several hundred *li* away to find work in the city of Xinxiang, in Henan province.

That was one of the most difficult periods of my life, and every time I think of it, I immediately burst into tears.

I had an uncle, my father's younger brother, who had left home and was working in a cement factory in Xinxiang. Because he was already there, Fourth Uncle introduced me to First Uncle's second son—which is to say, my elder cousin Shucheng. Shucheng was working as a porter in the Xinxiang train station, where he would unload coal or sand from the trains, load it onto a large cart, and then push the cart to the cement factory, more than thirty *li* away. He would get up when it was still dark and make one trip a day, transporting one ton—or a thousand *jin*—every trip. For every round trip of sixty-plus *li*, he could make four or five yuan. Because my cousin was already doing this work, I was able to secure a position when I arrived and also began working as a porter.

I was somewhat taller than my cousin but didn't have his stamina. Every day at dawn, the two of us would get up, take our empty carts, and hurry over to the train station more than thirty *li* away. There, each of us would load up a ton of coal or sand and, like oxen, haul the carts back to the factory. Where the ground was flat, we proceeded forward at a slow and halting pace, but when we encountered a hill, regardless of whether it was a gentle slope or a steep incline, we would leave one cart at the base of the hill, then work together to pull the other cart up the hill, zigzagging in an S-shaped trajectory. After successfully getting one load to the top, we would rest for a while and then go back down to retrieve the other one. In the summer, when it was as hot as an oven, our sweat would pour down like rain, but fortunately there were countless irrigation wells by the side of the road, and when we were overcome with thirst, we could lie down next to a roadside field and begin lapping up water like a horse, cow, or desert camel. By midday, we would reach the mouth of a well, where we would eat some steamed buns weighing four *liang* each—which, because they were hard and long, we nicknamed "poles." Whenever we stopped for water, my cousin and I would each eat two of those four-*liang* pole buns.

Initially, I couldn't pull that one-ton cart nor could I finish those two pole buns. My cousin became anxious on my behalf, and in addition to helping me every time we reached a hill, whenever we stopped to eat he would also give me a jet-black piece of pickled vegetable from a bag hanging from the handle of his cart. He would take a piece and eat one-third of it, then he would hand me the other two-thirds of that jet-black piece of pickled vegetable, so that together with the roadside water I had something to accompany those rock-hard pole buns. We continued in this way for a while, and when my cousin saw that I was able to finish two pole buns myself, he stopped giving me the pickled vegetables, and instead he would offer only some simple and deep observations about life.

He said, "Lianke, you should return home to resume your studies. Studying is a proper pursuit."

He said, "It's okay not to continue school, because if you study too much, it won't necessarily be useful."

He said, "Tomorrow is the weekend, so we should go back and take a bath. After bathing, you can have a good night's sleep."

Every Sunday, I would have a good night's sleep, attempting to regain the strength I had expended over the preceding week. However, even as my cousin urged me to rest, every Sunday he would still go down to the train station and haul an extra load of coal or sand.

My cousin and I were staying in the cement factory dormitory. Each Sunday, my cousin would leave with his cart, while I would continue lying in the empty room, disappointedly staring up at the ceiling, at a spider and the web that kept growing day-by-day. One day, I remembered the novel of which I had written several hundred pages. Sitting with my luggage, the manuscript appeared lonely and helpless. It had come with me to Xinxiang, but I hadn't had a chance to add a single detail since I arrived. In fact, I hadn't written even a single Chinese character.

I continued in this way for two more months. One day, however, Fourth Uncle noticed I was walking somewhat unevenly, with one shoulder higher than the other. He asked why, and I replied that I had always walked like this. My cousin bowed his head for a while and then looked up and said it was from pulling the cart. He explained that because I had to tie the shaft belt to my shoulder every day and then pull with all my strength, it ended up forcing one of my shoulders down.

After my cousin finished speaking, Fourth Uncle didn't say a word. Instead, his eyes filled with tears.

Three days later, Fourth Uncle prohibited me from returning to the train station to continue working as a porter. He said that regardless of how much money I might be able to earn, I shouldn't go back. He said that if I ruined my body, he would incur a debt to his elder brother and sister-in-law that he'd never be able to repay. He then invited a certain individual for drinks and a couple of meals, after which he was able to arrange for me to go to the cement factory's stone mountain, where I could drill and explode stone, and bring the fragments back to the factory in a mine car. There was real danger involved in this process; every month there would be instances of workers suffering lesions or crushed bones, or even dying in explosions. Given these safety concerns, Fourth Uncle also told my cousin to stop working as a porter and instead go with me to work on the mountain, so that we could help look after one another.

My cousin and I sold our carts and went to do piecework for the cement factory. The mountain range was located three to five *li* from the factory, and there were rail tracks connecting them. A winch and a steel wire were used to haul several mine cars up the mountain, and after they were filled with stones, the mine cars were quickly and steadily propelled back down the mountain by the force of gravity. Up on the mountain, the workers were divided into different groups; some were drilling with explosives, others loading the stones onto steel carts and pushing them a few hundred meters until the stones could be transferred to the mine cars, while others were responsible for guiding the mine cars down the mountain. Upon first arriving on the mountain, new workers would start out by doing three days of light work guiding the mine cars down the mountain. Once they had had a chance to familiarize themselves with their surroundings, the new workers would then be assigned to do more dangerous and exhausting work, such as planting explosives or moving stones.

I spent six days guiding the mine cars.

My cousin had passed on to me the three days of guiding the mine cars that he originally had been allotted. As soon as he arrived on the mountain he immediately began performing the hardest work of drilling blasting holes. Work on the mountain was assessed based on time, not output. Eight hours a day was considered one shift, and the wage for each shift was one yuan and sixty cents. In order to be assigned two shifts a day, thereby earning three yuan and two cents, my cousin and I went to see the foreman and spoke to him for a long time. Fourth Uncle sent the foreman two cartons of cigarettes and a bottle of *baijiu*, and as a result my cousin and I were permitted to work double shifts on the mountain, sixteen hours a day. Often we would work continuously for ten days or two weeks without ever coming down off the mountain, without bathing, and without entering the factory. We would eat and sleep on that empty mountain, and we would continue in this way until it rained, at which point we would finally be able to rest a little.

Although this life was extremely arduous, every month when I collected my salary and was able to send some money home, I would feel a limitless warmth and satisfaction as I emerged from the post office and gazed up at the sky and the passersby. I felt that I was now an adult and could assume some responsibility for supporting my parents and my family. A feeling of sweetness and pride would emerge from the depths of my heart, particularly when I received letters from my family saying that they had received the funds and that they had been just enough to allow them to undertake some necessary task or pay some debt. Upon hearing this, I would feel that I possessed an indomitable strength. Consequently, I developed an even greater desire to work and earn more money, which is why I became increasingly eager to work sixteen hours a day, even though it would mean working continuously for all those hours without any breaks.

The longest continuous stretch I spent on the mountain was forty-one days, working sixteen hours every day. This entire time I didn't wash my face or brush my teeth. Every day when I finished work I would immediately fall asleep, and when I woke up I would symbolically run a moist towel over my face, then rush back to the work site. Given that the factory was simultaneously pursuing revolution and promoting production, the order had been given that it should operate at full speed for a hundred days to produce tens of thousands of tons of cement that would support construction wherever it was needed. The entire factory was working nonstop, day and night, which naturally gave me the perfect opportunity to work double shifts without having to ask anyone's permission or give anyone gifts.

During this period there was an amusing incident that had implications for state secrets and the relations between the mainland and the island across the Taiwan Strait.

At the time, people in Mainland China knew two things about Taiwan: first, that the Taiwanese people all lived in a state of deep misery; and second, that we "will definitely liberate Taiwan" and rescue the Taiwanese people. Of course, even as we were determined to liberate them, the Taiwanese people had not given up their goal of subjugating us, and at any moment they were prepared to attack the mainland and seize our revolutionary regime. Therefore, at that time—and I don't know whether this was true or not—the mainland was full of KMT (Nationalist Party) spies from Taiwan, or so it seemed. For as long as I could remember, I was hearing stories about KMT spies, which made me suspect that our neighbors, one of my teachers, and many people wearing uniforms in the street were

KMT spies sent over from Taiwan. It reached the point that I could be walking alone through the fields on the edge of the village and would think I could hear footsteps behind me, whereupon I'd begin to suspect that it was a Taiwanese spy who was following me and deliberately matching my pace. When I spun around, I'd invariably find that behind me was nothing but an empty expanse.

In order to prove to myself that no one was following me, sometimes I'd walk quickly for several steps, then hide behind a wall or a tree. I would peek out and survey my surroundings, and after having confirmed that no spy was tailing me, I would carefully continue walking again. When I recall many incidents from that period, it is as though I'm recalling an old revolutionary movie—parts of which are now indistinct, while others remain very clear. There are many scenes featuring a vast historical void, but there are also many in which within that void there appear tiny details like wildflowers. It was a revolutionary era and a passionate one, in which revolution engendered passion, and passion could foment revolution. During these days, when I was working sixteen-hour double shifts on the mountain, I forgot everything, as though I had been completely cut off from the rest of the world. But it was precisely when I was in this state of isolation that great developments involving the revolution and the liberation of Taiwan came to a head.

The incident occurred in the afternoon. We were in the process of loading the mining car with crushed stone when the construction site suddenly had an electrical short. The mine car was unable to move, the pneumatic drill was unable to turn, and the workers— who, like me, were doing piecework in an attempt to earn enough to survive—all lay down on the crushed stones and promptly fell asleep. At this time, just as I was about to fall asleep, I saw two enormous pink balloons floating across the sky into the mountains.

As I watched those two balloons, my first thought was that they might have been sent by the KMT to distribute anti-revolutionary leaflets. As for whether a balloon from Taiwan could actually cross the Taiwan Strait, or where the Taiwan Strait was even located, or how many thousands of *li* it was from Fujian and Xiamen (the closest part of the mainland to Taiwan) over to Xinxiang here in Henan province—I had no idea, nor did I even have any interest in knowing. But as I watched that pair of balloons, I became increasingly convinced that they must have come from distant and deeply distressed Taiwan. In order to confirm my suspicion, while everyone was still half-asleep, I pretended I needed to go to the restroom and then left the construction site.

I looked in the direction in which the balloons had disappeared half an hour earlier. Then I proceeded from the mountaintop down to the uninhabited valley below, and it was only after I was convinced that the balloons had in fact drifted away and that I wouldn't be able to find them, that I finally stopped walking. However, just as I was turning around to return to the mountaintop, a miraculous scene suddenly appeared before my eyes.

I saw an object wedged between some stones on the side of the road. It looked like a bookmark; it was about four fingers wide and one hand span long and was printed elegantly on glossy paper. On one side was a beautiful young woman wearing a short skirt, and in each arm she was holding two children. Of her four children, two were boys and two were girls, and they were all healthy and adorable, carrying school bags and holding toys. In the background of this color photograph was a broad Taipei street, flanked on either side by tall buildings and streetlights. On the back of the card there was a bold line, printed in blue, which read:

TAIWAN HAS NO FAMILY-PLANNING POLICY

At that time, I was not yet very familiar with the phrase *family-planning policy*—a phrase that all peasants would later come to know all too well. I just guessed that this phrase had something to do with having children. During that period, our rural region had not yet implemented a family-planning policy, and it was only in some of China's cities that anyone had started to hear this call. So I was not particularly interested in family planning and simply felt that this card corroborated my suspicion that those balloons must have come from Taiwanese anti-revolutionaries. Upon seeing the card, I decided that, although the Taiwanese might be anti-revolutionaries, the beauty of their streets and their people was greater than anything I had ever imagined. I became deeply envious of the happy lives of the mother and children in the photograph.

The valley was vast and uninhabited. I took the card and quietly headed back up to the construction site. I hid that card in a crevice in the rocks, where the rain wouldn't reach it and no one would notice it. Although later I didn't dare go back to look at the card, I had already hidden in my heart a secret that I couldn't tell anyone, which was that it was entirely possible that in Taiwan the people led better lives than we did, and that it was actually we who were living in misery. This vague suspicion about society, revolution, and the world reminded me of my novel because the plot was full of class struggle and also featured a scene involving a spy from Taiwan.

I once again began working on the manuscript.

By that point my cousin had returned home to get married, so he had left me a single room in the factory. One day when I sat down to write, I noticed that, while I was hauling stones and a sledgehammer up the mountain every day, and then shoveling gravel onto carts, the shovel handle had been pressing on the fingers of my right hand, and as a result my fingers had become as crooked as twigs. No matter how hard I tried, I found that I could no longer hold the smooth and slick pencil. I stared at my hardened fingers and found myself completely at a loss. I wanted to weep but at the same time became very calm. I tried using my left hand, but I still couldn't write, and in the end I had no choice but to clasp the pencil with my right hand and stiffly begin to write until my characters once again started to resemble characters.

I stopped working double shifts and instead, after completing a single eight-hour shift, would close my door and spend several hours writing pages of my novel. I no longer held much hope that this work would ultimately be published and change my fate. Instead, I simply felt that while reality gave me a feeling of existential hopelessness, in writing I believed that a new world was possible.

In this way, I would work and write, write and work. If I was working a day shift, I'd write at night, and if I was working a night shift, I'd write during the day. At one point a large number of workers from other provinces suddenly left the construction site, and I once again had a chance to start working double shifts, but after another half month, the world turned upside down.

This process began late one night. It was already past midnight when the silence on the mountain was abruptly broken by loud music, which began playing over the construction site loudspeaker. The music was from the popular Henan opera *Chaoyang Valley*. Previously, that loudspeaker, apart from being used to broadcast announcements, had been used only to broadcast revolutionary news and revolutionary model operas. But that night, when there were clouds in the sky and everything was quiet, the loudspeaker suddenly started blaring the decadent and intoxicating sound of *Chaoyang Valley*. We didn't know why the loudspeaker had stopped broadcasting revolutionary model operas and instead switched to a beautiful local opera. Everyone stopped what they were doing and stared in surprise as they listened to the beautiful line "one step forward, two steps back, I might as well stop walking." After a while the older workers began to sing along.

That night the beauty of Henan opera suddenly dawned on me, and to this day I remain fascinated by this local musical tradition. Because I was scheduled to work a double shift that night, I didn't get off work until eight o'clock the next morning, and by the time I returned to the workers' dormitory at the base of the mountain it was already past noon. That day I saw countless bizarre slogans posted along the streets where the dormitory was located, and they all involved the toppling of Wang, Zhang, Jiang, and Yao: the "Gang of Four." At that point I didn't know who Wang, Zhang, Jiang, and Yao were, nor did I know what Gang of Four meant, just as I didn't know what "family planning" meant. When I returned to the dormitory, I asked Fourth Uncle who Wang, Zhang, Jiang, and Yao were.

Fourth Uncle explained that they were Wang Hongwen, Zhang Chunqiao, Jiang Qing, and Yao Wenyuan. I knew that Wang Hongwen, Zhang Chunqiao, Jiang Qing, and Yao Wenyuan were our country's great political leaders, and I remembered how, not long before, I had been working on the mountain and it wasn't until I came down a week later that I learned that Chairman Mao had died. Now, Chairman Mao's widow, Jiang Qing, and her friends had all been arrested, but it wasn't until much later that I dimly began to intuit that the world was undergoing a radical transformation. An astonishing new revolution was imminent, although all sorts of revolutions seemed to have no relationship to me. At the time, however, my first thought was that someone must have listed Wang, Zhang, Jiang, and Yao in the wrong order, because Jiang Qing's name should obviously have come first. Although Wang Hongwen was the nation's vice chairman, Jiang Qing was, after all, Chairman Mao's wife.

Later it was confirmed that China was, in fact, undergoing a new revolution.

And what was more, I was right—this revolution had nothing to do with me.

On a very ordinary day, when I was working on the mountain, Fourth Uncle urgently came up to see me. After a hesitation, he said, "You should go buy a train ticket to return home; there has been an emergency." I stood in front of him, staring in shock, feeling both alarmed and flustered. Fourth Uncle saw my distress, so he took out a telegram and slowly handed it to me.

The telegram contained only four words: *Emergency. Return Home Immediately*. At that time, the telephone network was not like it is today, covering everywhere like an endless web, making the world seem as small as a man's fist. At that time, the primary mode of communication was letter or telegram. For nonurgent matters we used letters, and for urgent matters, like family emergencies, we used telegrams. Because each Chinese character in a telegram cost six or eight cents, the equivalent of the cost of two or three eggs, telegrams tended to use the most abbreviated and disconcerting language possible.

Because our family had an invalid at home, I didn't dare think about what might lie behind the telegram. Instead, I simply grabbed the message and rushed down the mountain. I bought a train ticket, packed my things, and set out in the middle of the night, heading back to my home in Luoyang's Song county.

It was only upon arriving that I saw with my own eyes that everyone at home was safe, and the emergency was that society itself had undergone an unprecedented transformation.

6. THE UNIVERSITY ENTRANCE EXAMS

China's university entrance examination system had been reinstated.

Anyone, no matter who they were, could register to take the exams that could transform their destiny.

When I returned from Xinxiang, there were still four days until the exams. Because I hadn't graduated from high school, all I could do was dig up my middle-school textbooks and study nonstop for four days. Then, together with some classmates from the village, I went to a school several *li* away to take entrance exams that, for me, were still very alien. It was like seizing the opportunity to take a quick bite to eat and then rushing down the road of life toward my destiny.

I can't recall the contents of that year's exam, but I do remember the topic of the assigned essay: "My heart soars over to the Chairman Mao Mausoleum." This title was filled with a tragic and spectacular revolutionary sentiment. I clearly remember how in that essay, I described how I had stood on a terrace field that I had built myself, gazing out in the direction of Beijing's Tiananmen Square gate, thinking about Chairman Mao's glory and greatness. I did my best to express the sublime emotion I felt for the great leader. Because of my work on my novel, I was able to compose a long essay that appeared both thoughtful and intense. The instructions were to write around a thousand characters, and everyone was given three sheets of draft paper with four hundred squares each. I, however, wrote five pages. When I ran out of draft paper, I raised my hand to ask the teacher serving as examination proctor for more, which greatly surprised him. He lifted up my essay and announced, "Look at this student, able to write such a long essay, and furthermore with such excellent penmanship and smooth prose—he will definitely be able to pass the exams and be admitted to the university." The proctor added that he hoped other students would follow my example. I didn't know where that proctor was from, but his words led all the other students to look at me—the way that, at another moment in history, everyone's eyes had been focused on Beijing's Tiananmen Square gate.

But that year I didn't get into university.

In fact, no one from our entire county got a university place that year. A few students happened to get into a local teachers college, but out of the several hundred students in my examination site, it was hard to find one who was even accepted to a polytechnic school. One reason for this collective failure is that when everyone went to register for the exam, none of us knew the names of any of China's universities, the province's teachers colleges, or Luoyang's polytechnic schools. When we asked the teacher responsible for overseeing the application process what schools we should put down on our registration form, the teacher had replied, "You can put down anything."

We said, "But even if we just put down anything, it still needs to be the name of a school."

The teacher replied, "Then just write Peking University and Henan University."

We said, "We know Peking University is in Beijing, but where is Henan University?"

The teacher said, "Maybe it's in Zhengzhou." (In fact, it's in Kaifeng.)

Everyone immediately realized the problem. Every student wished to select Peking University as his or her first choice, because it was situated in the country's capital, the political and revolutionary center, a sacred site to which all Chinese are oriented. Eventually, someone took the lead and filled in Peking University, after which everyone followed suit.

I did the same.

Of course, not a single one of us was accepted.

Many students who took the exam with me repeated it the following year. As for me, I didn't do the rereading or the reexamination, nor did I return to Xinxiang to continue doing piecework for the cement factory. I wanted to stay home and finish my novel.

Fortunately First Uncle's eldest son, my cousin Facheng, was a celebrated craftsman and had established a small construction team. So during the day I went with him to remove bricks and ashes, training to be a mason, and at night I would go home and work on my novel. I continued in this way until New Year's Eve, when I wrote until the fireworks sounded the next day.

In the latter half of 1978, I finally finished my novel, but by the end of the year I began to entertain dreams of joining the army. In the journey of my life, this was the most significant step in my attempt to get to the city and pursue a new life. In the army, however, whenever people asked me why I wanted to be a soldier, I would always say that it was for the sake of the revolution—in order to protect my family and defend the nation. When they asked me why I wrote, I didn't say that this was my fate but rather that I was trying to increase my cultural status for the sake of the revolution, so that I could attempt to become a cultured and revolutionary soldier. Revolution was the root of that era. At the same time, revolution also concealed and buried everything else from that era.

Later, a local political leader heard that I liked to write, and when he expressed interest in seeing some of my work, I quickly called home long-distance, asking my brother to send him the three-hundred-thousand-character novel that I had spent several years writing. The next day my brother called me back and said, in despair, "Brother, after you left to join the army, Mother used your manuscript for kindling when she cooked, and also to light the stove in winter. She burned it up page by page."

I asked, "So, the entire thing was incinerated?"

He replied, "Yes, the entire thing."

CHAPTER 3

Missing My Father

1. SHADOWS OF THE SOIL

It has already been twenty-five years since Father left us.

Twenty-five springs and autumns is truly a long period of time. As this river of time flows past, there are countless things I'll never be able to forget, no matter how hard I try. The memory that is freshest in my mind is that of my father and the way he looked when he was engaged in manual labor. My father was a peasant, and work was his duty. Only by working day and night could he feel truly alive and believe that his life had significance. Work, for him, was an absolute necessity.

When I was small—only a few years old, not yet old enough to go to school—I would follow Father around the way a dog is followed by its tail. When he was working, I liked to stand next to him and step on his shadow as I watched him wield his various farm tools.

That was many, many years ago. At the time, every family still had its own land, and while the land belonging to the people's

communes was under public jurisdiction, every family was nevertheless allowed to keep one or more plots to use as they wished. In
addition, you were also permitted to cultivate any barren wasteland
and use it to plant melons or beans, trees or scallions. That was your
right, your freedom. Our family's plot was located on the rear slope
of a mountain several *li* from our house. The plot faced the sun,
but the soil was of poor quality and full of brownish-yellow ginger
stones. This was known as ginger-stone soil, and every time a hoe or a
shovel entered the soil, it would invariably hit ginger stones that were
neither round nor square, and which had neither angles nor edges.
Whenever we tried to plow this plot, we would break our plowshare,
again and again. So, in order to be able to cultivate this soil, Father
spent several winter rest seasons taking the entire family out to the
plot to repeatedly turn the soil, rain or shine. He would use a hoe
to dig down a foot, and then would remove all the ginger stones he
found. My sisters and I would take the large and thin stones to the
front of the field, so that we could carry them with us when it was
time to return home. Back home, we would pile the stones beneath
our house, so when it was time to build a new house, we could use
the stones to construct the foundation or a gable wall. As for the
stones that were too small or shapeless to use for construction, we
would either leave them on the side of the field or else dump them
into the ravine, so that the wind and rain could mercilessly punish
them for their uselessness.

Father was more than 1.7 meters tall, and while these days this
might not be considered particularly extraordinary, several decades
ago it was extremely rare to find someone his height in the countryside. I would watch him as he lifted his hoe over his head, with the
blade facing the sky. On a clear day, the blade would look as though
it could almost slice the sun in half and on a cloudy day cut through
the clouds. Because we were the only family working on that side

of the mountain, our surroundings were remarkably quiet, and all I could hear was the pattering sound of Father's hoe cutting through the clouds. Following that sound, I would see his hoe freeze for a moment in midair, and then he would bring it down again, burying it deep in the hard soil. When he bent his hips, dust would fly from his white clothes, as though kicked up by a departing car. Father hoed and hoed, and time would flow under his hoe and disappear. One winter day after another, the soil would be broken apart and then would clump back together again. I could see clearly that when he went up the mountain, his hips would be as straight as a rail, but by afternoon they would resemble a tree weighed down by a heavy load—the tree would still be standing, but it would be markedly bent. After Father had eaten lunch up on the mountainside, this tree would appear as though it had been relieved of its load and would struggle to straighten up again. But by late afternoon it would be bent almost double, as though weighed down by an even heavier load, and it would look like it could never straighten again. Nevertheless, Father would lift his hoe over and over again, forcefully bringing it down onto those stones, and would continue doing so until the sun had completely disappeared.

At that point, I'd say, "Father, the sun has already set."

Father would lift his hoe and look to the west, then ask, "Has it?"

I would reply, "Look . . . it's already set."

Every time I said this, Father would act as though he didn't believe the sun had really set. He would stare at me and then gaze out at the western mountains. After confirming that the sun had indeed set and that dusk had fallen, he would bring down his hoe one final time. After breaking apart one last ginger stone, he would drop his hoe and, with his hands firmly at his waist, would lean backward—so that his exhausted back, which had been bent over all day, could release some refreshing popping sounds. Then he would turn and look for a pile of soil or packed earth where he could lie down facing the sky. He would lie down so the pile of soil or dirt was pressing directly against his hip bones. Casually and dexterously, he would use the soil as a mattress, and while breathing evenly he would grab several handfuls of wet soil and knead them into a ball, then break them apart again. After repeating this process several times, he would stand up and gaze out at all the soil he had turned over, and with even steps he would walk back and forth east and west, north and south. After making several measurements, he would take a stick and scrawl out some calculations in the dirt. With a face as red as clay, he would produce a faint yet bright laugh.

I would ask, "How much land is there?"

Father would reply, "Sufficient to grow enough soy beans for our family, but if we want to raise sweet potatoes we'll need to dig a storage cave."

Then, with loads of stones on our carrying poles, we would proceed down the mountain and head home. Although those ginger stones were not as hard and heavy as river stones, they were nevertheless still rocks, and to stand up with his load, Father would have to lean on the hoe handle. But on his way down the mountain he'd stop only once or twice to rest. You could see where his drops of sweat had fallen to the ground, creating small, bean-like depressions in the dust, like raindrops that quickly evaporated under the rays of the setting sun. I followed him down, carrying the hoe he had been using all day. The hoe was so heavy it felt like it was pressing me into the ground, and I longed to throw it aside. Although I was falling farther and farther behind, I could still clearly hear Father's spine creaking under his load of stones. I had no choice but to switch the pole to the other shoulder and jog up to him, to avoid losing him.

When we got home, Father would place his load of ginger stones beneath the house's gable and then collapse onto the pile. If it wasn't too late and it wasn't too cold outside, he would sit there while my sisters brought out their rice bowls, and only after they were done eating dinner would he get up and go inside, formally concluding his day's work. I always doubted whether Father, who by that point would be sound asleep, would be able to wake the next morning, but without fail he would always get up the next day and take me and the rest of the family back up to the mountainside to continue turning the soil.

We continued in this manner for three years—for three long winters—until all the soil in our family's plot of land was successfully turned. By this point the pile of ginger stones under our house's gable was sufficient to build two more gables for our three-room house, while the pile in the ravine at the front of the field was sufficient to build several more houses. You simply wouldn't believe how many ginger stones were in that small plot of land. When you saw them you finally realized that our self-cultivated plot, which was several times larger than it had originally appeared, had been derived largely from the gaps between the stones. Altogether, it was perhaps seven- or eight-tenths of a *mu*, or even an entire *mu*, in size, but for me at the time, that plot of land was like a town square—smooth, soft, and exuding a sweet red smell of soil. You could begin tumbling and turning somersaults in that field, and you still wouldn't encounter anything hard. Through that field I realized that for a peasant, all joy and bitterness in life was grounded in the land, that everything was intimately connected to labor.

Beginning that summer, the edges and corners of that plot underwent a fundamental transformation, as the uneven areas along the borders were covered with a stone wall, and thornbushes were planted along the edge of the plot facing the road to prevent goats and oxen from wandering in. We hoed parts of the field that were so angular as to be completely unplowable and then placed a mushroom-like pile of sweet potatoes there. During the sweltering summer, we would fetch water from the base of the mountain several *li* away, and that plot of land produced its first season of sweet potato sprouts.

Perhaps it was that Father's labor impressed heaven and earth, but for whatever reason, the weather that year was excellent, and the plot's sweet potatoes grew particularly well. In the process of collecting the ginger stones we had also dug up all the weeds by their roots and thrown them away, so other than luscious green sweet potato sprouts, the plot had barely any vegetation. Of all the peasants who walked past, there wasn't a single one who didn't stop and stare, and if Father happened to be working there, he would smile while hoeing the soil around the sprouts.

One passerby said, "Heavens, look how well your sprouts are growing!"

Father replied, "This is the first year I've planted crops here. Next year they won't grow as well."

The passerby said, "If our family doesn't have enough grain to make it through the winter, we'll ask you for some of your potatoes."

"Of course, of course."

In order to store the plot's sweet potatoes, Father expanded the storage cellar on the side of our house facing the village wall, and across from it he dug an even larger one. Once everything was ready, all we needed to do was to wait for the beginning of the First Frost solar term in early fall, at which point we would begin that season's harvest. For the harvest, Father asked a blacksmith to extend the blade of his hoe by an inch; then he bought a couple of peach-colored wicker baskets, and from the rafters he hung the twine he would use to tie up the potato stems. Everything was ready, and all we had to do was wait for the First Frost.

That year, the Cold Dew solar term began on October eighth or ninth, while the First Frost began half a month later. But on the first day of the Cold Dew, the local production brigade convened a mass meeting at which the village branch secretary announced a red-letter directive that had been sent down from the central authorities to the provincial capital and from the provincial capital to the district and county seats, and on down to the branch secretaries of each production brigade. The directive specified that the people's communes were not allowed to permit individual families to own their own land, and within three days of receiving this directive, each family had to return all of its self-cultivated land to the collective.

This was in 1966.

At noon on the first day of the Cold Dew solar term, Father didn't eat after returning home from the meeting, and instead he sat in the doorway, his face deathly pale. He stared out into space, not saying a word. Mother brought him a bowl of soup, and asked, "What are we going to do? Will we really hand over our land?"

Father didn't respond.

Mother repeated, "Are we not going to hand it over?"

Father glanced at her, and then asked in response, "Do we have a choice? How could we dare not to?"

After saying this, Father looked at the bowl Mother had brought him. He didn't accept it and instead walked out of the house alone. Father still hadn't returned by the time we finished lunch, nor had he returned by dinnertime. We all knew where he had gone, and we wanted very much to bring him back, but Mother said we should leave him for a while. In the end, after night had fallen and the sky was completely dark, Father finally returned home, utterly exhausted. When he arrived, he was carrying a bundle of sweet potato sprouts from which were dangling several large red sweet potatoes. After putting down his load, Father said to Mother, "That plot of ours has rich soil and is facing the sun, and the *fengshui* is also very good. You know, it would make an excellent tomb. When someone dies, they could be buried there."

When we heard Father say this, the entire family fell silent.

We remained silent until after the moon had set and the stars had faded.

2. BUILDING A HOUSE

No one could have anticipated that Father would pass away so abruptly. My mother, brother, sisters, and neighbors all felt he left the world much too early. However, from the day Father first fell ill, he seemed to understand an important truth—which was that for healthy people, death is always standing at the end of your life waiting for you to approach, step-by-step and day-by-day. It waits until you are right in front of it and it can reach out to you, at which point it will grasp you and take you away. But for an invalid, not only are you continually approaching death, step-by-step and day-by-day, but death is continually running toward you, step-by-step and day-by-day. Human life is that finite distance between you and death, and if you progress at a certain pace, it will take you a fairly long period of time to reach death. But if death moves toward you while you simultaneously progress toward it, then your life will be significantly shorter than it would have been otherwise. In this world, everyone has this journey, and if someone finishes the journey on his own, that is one thing, but if death's invisible shadow is rushing toward you down life's path, then that is another matter altogether. My father must have understood this truth early on. Because he had been ill, he must have glimpsed his future journey into that invisible world and must have seen that a dark shadow was already rushing toward him. And so, as a peasant and a father, he was very anxious to make sure that he carried out all of his obligations in this world before he died.

What kinds of things did Father, as a peasant living in this world, have to achieve before his death? What responsibilities did he have to fulfill? Father was like all other northern peasants, all northern men, and all the peasants around him who were fathers and who never traveled farther than the county seat a few dozen *li* away. If they were able to make it to Luoyang, more than a hundred *li* away, this would surely constitute a real achievement. From the day they became fathers, they knew in their hearts that their biggest, most solemn responsibility was to build houses for their sons and prepare dowries for their daughters, so that they could see their children get married and establish their own families. For virtually all peasant fathers, this was their primary ambition in life—perhaps their only ambition.

I thought that, because of his illness, Father must have perceived this objective even more clearly, strongly, and simply. He must have felt that the most urgent task he needed to complete before he died was to arrange his children's weddings.

An ideal wedding, however, was predicated on having a house. Whenever a family had a house, the family's children would have the necessary foundation for an ideal marriage. A house was a propitious sign and the symbol of a peasant's household. Indeed, in any village a good house was always a symbol of the family's social position. Father therefore invested virtually all of his energy and wealth into an attempt to build a tile-roofed house for his sons.

I no longer remember how our family's first three-room tile-roofed house was built. All I remember is that the walls were made from packed earth, and the one facing the street was layered with yellow ginger stones that we had painstakingly brought back from the mountainside field, while the remaining three were coated in a layer of mud mixed with wheat bran. Every spring, countless emaciated wheat sprouts would grow out of the latter three walls. I remember how the semicircular tiles were arranged in rows on the house's roof, and how from every direction they looked like flocks of geese suspended motionless in the sky, in the shape of the character for *human*: 人. I remember how everyone who passed by—men and women, young and old—would stop and scrutinize that three-room tile-roofed house, as though studying a new technique for raising crops. Just as when they passed by my father's self-cultivated plot years earlier, their faces would light up with an envious glow and silent praise. I still remember how, after I moved into that tile-roofed house, Mother would smile and tell me and my siblings how, before building the house, she and Father had gone to a forest deep in the mountains more than two hundred *li* away and had proceeded to drag countless wooden logs out of the wolf-infested gully and up to the roadside. To this day Mother continues to describe how, during the Lunar New Year holiday of the year when our family began building the house, we didn't have even a grain of wheat or handful of flour and therefore had to borrow a bowl of dirty wheat flour so that my three siblings and I could each have half a bowl of dumplings, and how my parents didn't eat a single dumpling that year. Mother would also recount how she tried to make white flour go further by combining it with red sweet potato flour, so that she could make her children more cabbage-filled dumplings, but after trying several times, she discovered that this wouldn't work because the sweet potato flour wasn't thick enough. Instead she just covered the sweet potato flour paste with a layer of white flour and gave it to Father for his New Year's dinner.

This is the earliest memory that I have of that house. All I remember from afterward is what I saw—which was our newly built three-room, tile-roofed house. But because the house was too rickety and constantly leaked, every year during the rainy season, we had to place basins and pots to catch the water. Father worked several years to renovate this leaky house, and in the end not only did he make it so that the house no longer leaked, he even installed brick columns in the corner of each of those packed-earth walls, and placed dark green bricks around the windows and door. He strengthened the gable facing the street and the house's front wall with a layer of long ginger stones, while each square meter of the ginger-stone wall was marked by an erect brick serving as a partition. This made the original packed-earth house look as though it had been dressed in a green-and-yellow shirt, which not only helped protect the earthen walls from rain but instantly made the house appear more beautiful. The renovated house attracted people's attention and made locals gaze at it with envy.

This was Father's dream.

It was also one of Father's most important goals in life, for which he felt he had to exert the utmost effort during his remaining time in this world. His illness had become life-threatening. For people today, asthma is no worse than a headache or a fever, but while headaches and fevers are commonplace symptoms that are usually easy to heal, asthma can worsen until it becomes an untreatable condition. In the countryside, and particularly in remote mountainous regions, it was almost inevitable that old people would suffer from this illness. When people were young they would work in freezing conditions, and they frequently caught colds. By the time they reached their fifties or sixties, more than half of them would have developed asthma, and it was quite common for them to eventually die from it. Over his lifetime, Father had witnessed too many instances of people departing from this world on account of complications from asthma. He understood that if you contracted this illness, you would have to rely on your youthful body and soul, and hope that you would have the good fortune to recover; otherwise, you would suffer the same fate as the others.

The difference between Father and others, however, was that he wasn't yet thirty when he first fell ill. Given his youth and his general good health, at first he didn't worry much. When his asthma acted up, he borrowed some money to purchase a few doses of medicine and kept working nonstop as long as there was light outside. He continued in this manner for several years, day-after-day and month-after-month. Finally, before he had even turned fifty, the illness began returning every winter, leaving him like a seventy-year-old asthmatic. As a result, he wanted to finish building the house as quickly as possible, so that when his children grew up they could get married without delay. After each of us got married, he would consider he had carried out part of his heart's desire.

When my three siblings and I got married, our marriages unfolded under the watchful eye of our neighbors in the village, which is now a town. These neighbors thought that the entire process, from the initial engagement to the eventual marriage, unfolded very smoothly. Apart from the contributions of my mother and us siblings, this was due in no small part to Father's decision to endure hunger and illness in order to build the family a tile-roofed house. It was a small, 170-square-meter rural residence. Around the center, Father built three main rooms, and on each side he constructed two side rooms, making seven structures in all, with a forty-square-meter courtyard in the middle. In western Henan, this was considered the most fashionable and luxurious type of rural residence, and in order to save enough money to build it, Father rarely bought new clothes for New Year holiday. He planted paulownia and poplar trees in the front and at the back of the house. In the winter, he placed a layer of lime over the saplings and surrounded them with straw to keep them warm. When spring arrived, he removed the straw, the way that one might remove a child's heavy clothing. He planted thornbushes around each tree to prevent children from touching them with their hot hands. He raised the trees as one might raise one's own children, and years later, when the trees reached middle age, they would provide wood for the house's rafters.

Eventually our family's seven-room house was made into a tile-roofed one. Although Father wasn't the first villager to build a tile-roofed house, he was the first to build one in which not a single part of the structure—including even the chicken coop and the pigsty—had a thatched roof. When Father's asthma worsened, he would wear a yarn face mask to keep out the cold, but he would still pull a cart to look for stones and building materials along the river. We would then haul the stones back to pave the courtyard and the path leading to the outhouse and the pigsty, ensuring that the 170-square-meter complex didn't have a speck of dirt anywhere. Every time it rained, everyone else's houses became extremely muddy, and only ours remained immaculately clean. During that kind of weather, our courtyard would always become filled with neighbors, and in that immaculate courtyard and mud-free house, people would play cards, exchange stories, and discuss fate and mortality. In this way, our house was besieged with rural life and came to function as an example of our village architecture and a model for our village.

Our mansion and the life in it had a great influence and reputation in the village and surrounding communities and served as an inspiration for many peasants' lives. However, only a handful of close relatives knew that in order to achieve this, Father had sacrificed his health and cut short his life. I remember that after Father finally completed the residence's initial side rooms, he led us across the Yi River, breaking through ice to cross, and into the valley in order to find stones for the rest of the house's foundation. Because the cart was too full, it capsized in the river on our way back. My siblings and I rolled up our pants' legs and stood in the middle of the icy river, pushing the cart with all our might. However, not only were we unable to push it forward even half a step, but our hands and faces turned blue from the cold, and our legs and feet began trembling such that we could barely stand up. At this point, Father turned around and emerged from between the shafts of the cart. He led me and my sisters back to shore, and then wrapped our legs with padded clothing. Next, he went back into the water and, together with my elder brother, removed several stones weighing one or two hundred *jin* from the cart and used shoulder poles to carry them back to shore. Once half the stones had been removed, Father was finally able to pull the cart to shore. When he emerged from the water, the veins in his neck were throbbing and his head was soaked in sweat, even as his hands, shoulders, legs, and virtually every strip of clothing was covered in ice. We rushed into the river to help him, and after he pulled the cart to a dry spot on the riverbank, we noticed he was having trouble catching his breath—to the point that his face had turned blue. Upon seeing Father's blue and swollen face, Eldest Sister began pounding his back. After some time, he finally resumed his labored breathing, whereupon Elder Brother retrieved the final stone from the icy river. He placed it on the cart, then gazed at Father's face and said, "We don't need to build these additional two rooms. You shouldn't risk your life for this."

Father didn't immediately respond. Instead, he glanced at my brother, looked back at us, and then gazed out into the distance. He reflected for a while and seemed to reach a decision. He turned to us and said, "I should take advantage of the fact that my asthma is not yet too severe and I can still work, so I should quickly finish building the house. In a few years I'll no longer be able to work, and if at that time I haven't been able to give each of you a residence and haven't had a chance to see each of you get married and establish your own families, then I'll have let you down and will be ashamed of my life."

So, although Father's illness initially developed when he was still a young man, it wasn't until he was trying to build residences for his sons' marriages that it really started to take hold of him. I was the youngest of four siblings, and the construction of the final two-room tile-roofed residence for my marriage in October 1984 marked the completion of Father's final wish. Not long afterward, he left us for another world, to find a different kind of peace.

3. BEATINGS

It has been a quarter of a century since Father last spoke to me. The trunks of the willow trees in front of the mound of yellow earth where he was buried are now very thick. I don't know whether, over the past twenty-four or twenty-five years, he has missed me, my siblings, and my mother. And if he has missed us, then what specifically has he missed? Meanwhile, I have never stopped thinking about him. I remember how, when I was young, Father would sometimes curse and beat me, and it seems as if every time I think of him, I always start from those memories.

The first beating I can remember was when I was seven or eight years old and still in elementary school. At that time, every year before the Lunar New Year holiday, Father would collect some coins he had painstakingly saved up and ask an acquaintance to take them to the village to exchange them for a bundle of brand-new ten-cent bills. He would then place these bills beneath the reed cover of his pillow, and on the first day of the New Year holiday, he would give one bill to each of his children, his nieces and nephews, and the children of other relatives who visited during the first two weeks of the new year. But that particular year, when it came time for Father to give everyone the money, it turned out that there wasn't a single bill left of the several dozen ten-cent bills that had been there. This was because that year, I had discovered the new bills hidden beneath the reed mat, and also that on my way to school there was a store in which a relative sold sesame-seed cakes for ten cents each. Every morning, accordingly, I would surreptitiously remove a ten-cent bill from beneath the mat and use it to buy a sesame-seed cake on my way to school. Sometimes I would take two bills, so that I could buy a second sesame-seed cake on my way home. From New Year's Day to day five, Father didn't even give me a look, much less did he curse me or beat me. Instead, he let me enjoy the New Year's holiday as usual. On day six, he finally asked me whether I had stolen the money. I replied that I hadn't, whereupon he told me to kneel down. He asked again whether I had stolen the money, and I continued to insist that I hadn't, whereupon he slapped me. He asked me again, but when I continued to insist that I hadn't taken it, he slapped me even harder. I can't remember how many times he slapped me; I just remember that he kept beating me until I couldn't bear it anymore, and finally I confessed that I stole the money to buy sesame-seed cakes. Father then fell silent and looked away. I didn't know why he turned away and didn't look at me or at my siblings, but when he turned back to us, we saw that his eyes were full of tears.

The second time he beat me was also before I turned ten, after I went with several classmates to steal cucumbers from someone's field. If we had only stolen the cucumbers, Father might not have beaten me, or at least he might not have beaten me so badly. However, one of my classmates also stole all the money that the owner of the plot had earned that year from selling cucumbers. The plot's owner then visited each of our households, saying that if we had only eaten his cucumbers, that would be one thing, but that someone had also stolen all of his family's food money for the coming year, and if the money wasn't returned, his family wouldn't be able to survive the winter. Father apparently decided that I must have stolen the money, since by that point I already had a track record. So, after the other man left, Father closed the main gate to our house and ordered me to kneel down on the courtyard's stone-paved ground. After hitting me several times, he asked whether I had stolen the man's money. Because I really hadn't done it, I told him no. Father kept slapping my face until he was exhausted and panting heavily, and only then did he sit down and glare at me—and at my face, which was now as swollen as freshly plowed and aerated soil. Because I felt wronged, I skipped dinner that night and instead went directly to bed. I fell asleep as soon as I lay down.

In the middle of the night, however, Father woke me up and asked, in a plaintive tone, "Did you really not steal that man's money?" I nodded that I hadn't. And then . . . then Father gently caressed my face. Next, he turned aside, to gaze out through the window at the moon and the night sky. After a while, he walked out of the room. He went and sat down in the courtyard, sitting all alone on a bench on the stone-paved ground where he had made me kneel down. He gazed up at the sky, letting the dew moisten his face. I fell back asleep, and when I woke up later to go to the bathroom, I saw that Father was still there, now quietly kneeling, completely motionless.

At the time, I didn't know what Father was pondering as he was sitting there. Even now, several decades later, I still don't know whether he was reflecting on something profound or simply entertaining whatever thoughts came about our family and that other man.

The third time, I deserved a beating. Father should have beaten me until my nose was bruised, my face was swollen, and my head was bloody. But in the end, he didn't touch me. It was I who prevented him from beating me. At that time, I was already perhaps a teenager, and when I was playing, I went by the village administrative office and saw that in a village cadre's window, there was a razor in a beautiful aluminum case. I reached through the window and grabbed the case, then returned home and told my father I had found a razor set in the road.

Father asked, "Where was it?"

I said, "It was in the entrance to the village administrative office."

Father wasn't someone who always needed to get to the bottom of things, but neither was he born yesterday. Later, he used that razor for a long time. Every two or three days, whenever I saw him looking at the small mirror in the razor set, my heart would fill with a feeling of warmth, as though this were actually a present I had bought for him. I don't know why, but I never felt guilty on account of that genuine act of theft and never tried to speculate about that cadre from whom I had stolen the razor. It wasn't until several years later, when I returned home on a break after having joined the army, and I saw my sick father was still using that razor, that I started feeling a twinge of regret.

I told him, "You've been using this razor for many years. The next time I come home, I'll bring you a new one."

Father said, "No need. This one works just fine. It's so sturdy that you'll still be able to use it even after I die."

When I heard this, I wanted to weep—and as Father had that time when he was beating me years ago, I promptly turned away.

As I did so, I happened to see an old copy of the *Henan Daily* that had been pasted onto our house's outer wall, and the page in question included the table of contents for the second issue of 1981 of Zhengzhou's *Hundred Flower Garden* magazine. That table of contents, in turn, happened to include one of my own stories, "A Woman Receiving Subsidies." I told Father that my stories had been published and made headlines, and that the newspaper pasted on our house wall contained the title of one of them. Father turned his half-shaved face and looked at the section of the newspaper where I was pointing.

Less than three years later, Father died of natural causes. I returned home to arrange his funeral, and as I was straightening up his things I saw the razor with the aluminum case sitting on the windowsill. All the yellow paint that had decorated the case had peeled off, and the white aluminum was glittering in the sunlight. And on the wall kitty-corner to the window, below where my name appeared on the table of contents of *Hundred Flower Garden*, there was a large black smudge where the paper had been touched countless times, to the point that the characters for my name, Yan Lianke, were barely visible anymore.

It has now already been about a quarter of a century since Father left me. During that time, I've never stopped writing fiction nor have I stopped missing him, even the memories of when he beat me. It seems odd that, even today, Father's beatings still make me feel so happy and secure, such that every time I think of him I reflexively caress my son's head. During my father's life, it would have been good if he could have beaten me eight or ten times. I feel that if only Father could still curse and beat me today the way he used to, I would feel happy and secure.

4. LOSS OF FILIALITY

It hadn't occurred to me that next year, the thirteenth day of the eleventh lunar month will be the twenty-fifth anniversary of the day my father left this world. To tell the truth, over the past quarter century I have never once remembered to observe the anniversary of Father's death. Even when he was still alive I never remembered his birthday. As I sit down to record these reminiscences, I write the words *the thirteenth day of the eleventh lunar month*, followed by two blank boxes for the time, and hope that later I'll be able to make inquiries and fill in the blanks. As I stare at those two blank spaces, however, I suddenly realize how unfilial I've been and how much of a debt I owe my father.

When Father passed away twenty-five years ago, we placed his body in the front room of our house, on a straw-covered pallet we had fashioned from a wooden door. My elder brother and sisters and I kept vigil by the corpse—quietly watching our father, who had been unwilling to depart from this world of pain and suffering. I resolved that after burying Father, I would express my filiality by writing something about him, narrating his life and love of life—even if it was a short piece only about three hundred or five hundred characters long. After Father was buried, my wife and I left that poor village in Song county, in western Henan province, and moved to a military barracks in the ancient capital of Kaifeng, in eastern Henan. Yet as a result of my work and the joy of my new marriage, together with my devotion to writing fiction, the solemn promise I made while kneeling by my father's corpse slowly faded. I would periodically remember my broken promise and begin to feel somewhat uneasy, but then I would quickly console myself, saying, *I'll write something on the three-year anniversary of his death, which in rural custom is a very auspicious day.* But the three-year anniversary came and went, and one day I suddenly received a letter from my elder brother, saying that he, my eldest sister, and several of our other relatives had gone to add some fresh soil to Father's grave. It was only at that point that I began to feel a twinge of anxiety and guilt. During work that day, once all of my colleagues had left for lunch, I sat alone in the empty office, placed my brother's letter on the desk, and stared out the window at the winter scene of poplar trees, listening to the birdsong rushing between the tree branches. Occasionally, I heard the sound of falling leaves, like moonlight brushing by, as my tears left splotches on my brother's letter. It seemed as though time slowed down on account of my tears and my distress. I sat there quietly, feeling guilty and ashamed, until after lunch, when from the office building I could hear the bell that signaled the return to work, along with the sound of rushing feet. My two-year-old son crossed the courtyard to visit me in my office to tell me to eat—and only then was I roused from my stupor.

On my way home from my office, I looked at the fresh and lively world around me and at the other passersby, who were all full of energy. I missed Father, and I kept turning away to wipe my tears, caressing my son's head and telling myself, *Wait until the ten-year anniversary of Father's death, and if by that time I still haven't written anything about his life, and still haven't done anything to commemorate his memory, then I truly can't be considered his son and won't even deserve a good death!* Yet, after several more years passed, I found I still hadn't done anything to observe Father's birthday or the anniversary of his death, and I still hadn't written anything in his memory. I recalled the time I had walked along the banks of a dry riverbed and found that I couldn't remember how the river had previously rushed along and realized it was quite possible that I had forgotten him—which is to say, I had simply squeezed his life out of my memory to the point that I had come to view it as bleak and desolate. In fact, I even forgot it was his blood that was flowing through my veins and that it was he who had given me life, raised me to adulthood, and cultivated me so that I could establish a family and a career. I thought, if there is indeed justice in this world, then what should my punishment be for repeatedly breaking the promises I made to Father? How would he have regarded a son like me? Would he make sure that I wouldn't have a good death, as I had sworn in my oath? After I leave this earth, would he make me kneel down before him forever?

I thought perhaps he might—because the lack of filiality with which I had treated him had been simply too great and too deep.

On the other hand, perhaps he might not—because I was, after all, his son, and the boy whom he had raised. But now I have sat down to write, and in doing so I know I can use Father's life to reflect back on my own and attempt to come to terms with my virtues and vices, successes and failures. I will attempt to come to terms with this mortal world, including all births and deaths, its material successes and failures. I will do so until the river runs dry, until the tree leaves wither and fall, and until my life is extinguished and reborn, reborn and extinguished again.

5. ILLNESS

Father died of natural causes.

In that town of only a few thousand residents, virtually everyone knew that Father died of natural causes. He died from a combination of asthma and emphysema, which ultimately developed into pulmonary heart disease. But illness was really only the superficial cause of his death, and if you consider it carefully, the deeper, more fundamental cause of his premature demise was his anxiety over my and my siblings' future. That is to say, the most direct reason for his death was his endless concern for me, which was as high as a mountain and as deep as the sea.

In reality, my stubbornness was the root of Father's relapse and was what made him leave this world—and leave Mother and my siblings—when he was still only fifty-eight. In other words, it's quite possible it was my fault that Father prematurely had to bid his farewell to this world he loved so deeply, despite its hardships.

I was the one who cut short Father's life.

When I think back, it seems that during that period, our family was like countless others, in that we never had any truly bright days. At the time—around the beginning of the Cultural Revolution—China's countryside was in a continual state of famine. It seemed that ours was not the only household where on the Lunar New Year either there were no dumplings or else Mother would close the outer gate and secretly make dumplings with red sweet potato flour wrapped inside skins made from white flour. However, our family was unusual in that not only was Father struggling with asthma, but also my eldest sister had come down with her illness. In our 170-square-meter house, which Father had worked so hard to build, the red-and-green sound of my eldest sister's crying resembled an enormous forest canopy that was full of leaves all year round and obscured the sun—such that in the winter we couldn't see the sunlight and in the summer couldn't feel the wind. When I think back, it occurs to me that my sister's illness must have been the sort of avascular necrosis that now one often sees mentioned in street flyers. At the time, though, my family sold everything we could possibly sell—including our grain, vegetables, plants, eggs, and even the livestock on which we relied for our household income—in a desperate attempt to find someone who could diagnose and treat her illness. In the end, however, whether we went to the town's local clinic, the county hospital that peasants viewed as a disaster zone, or the People's Hospital in Luoyang, all we found were doctors shaking their heads in futility.

In their attempt to cure my sister's illness, my parents hauled her around in a cart from doctor to doctor. I have no idea how many pairs of shoes they wore out, how many roads they walked, or how many tears they shed. My family sold the lumber Father had been planning to use to build a house, the pigs that were not yet fully grown, and the chickens that were still laying eggs. At the age of fifteen, my elder brother went to work in a coal mine a hundred *li* away. At the age of fourteen, my second sister began taking a cart to a valley several *li* away to haul back sand and stones she could then sell to the town's highway department and cement factories for one and a half yuan per cubic meter. Meanwhile, by the age of thirteen, I was already working for a construction team and had become particularly adept at carrying bricks and removing ashes. For many years, our family put Father's illness aside and focused on trying to cure Eldest Sister. Everything—including farming, doing piecework, selling property, and all other assorted and sundry efforts—revolved around Elder Sister's illness. We couldn't afford to purchase blood plasma when Eldest Sister had her operations, so Father, Mother, Elder Brother, Second Sister, and I all waited in the hospital entrance to donate blood for her. I watched as Elder Brother extended his arm across a fly-covered table, and a cold and bright needle was inserted into his vein, and bright red blood flowed through a tube and dripped into a bottle. As the empty bottle filled with blood, Elder Brother's face went from black to light yellow and then from light yellow to white.

Finally, when the bottle was filled, the doctor looked at Elder Brother and said, "All of you have the blood type your sister needs, so why don't you let someone else from your family donate?"

Elder Brother replied, "Mother is weak and Father is ill, so let me do it."

The doctor said, "What about your younger brother?"

Elder Brother said, "Let me do it. My brother is young and also still has to work."

Then the doctor removed the needle from the full bottle and placed it into an empty one. That was in winter, and the sun was warm and clean, and as it shone down on the bottle, the blood inside glowed bright red, as foam and bubbles rose and fell inside. I think I was fourteen or fifteen that year. In any event, my youthful sensitivity had already begun sighing over its fate, like sprouts born in late autumn, which have to prematurely confront the arrival of winter's frost and snow, and before they are even fully grown find themselves enveloped in bitter cold. I watched as the bottle filled with fresh blood, and listened as the blood silently dripped down and bubbles on the sides of the bottle formed and dissolved under the bright sun. I looked at Elder Brother's face, which was as white as a sheet of paper. At that moment, I appreciated Elder Brother's extraordinary selflessness and dimly sensed that I would never be mentioned in the same breath as him.

That year, Eldest Sister's illness didn't improve at all.

During the several days before and after Lunar New Year, in order to help lessen the family's anxiety and add some joy to the household, and to help her parents and siblings have a festive holiday, Eldest Sister claimed that her illness had improved considerably. Afterward she hid in her room and didn't go out. When she was in pain, she would bite her lip until her face turned green, but she would be careful not to cry out. When she truly couldn't endure anymore, she'd duck out through the back courtyard and go to an area of the village where there was no one around, and there she would pull at her hair and bang her head against a wall. Then she would wait for the pain to pass, and then she would return home with a smile on her face, help Mother cook and serve Father some rice, and wash her younger siblings' clothes—as though in this way attempting to atone for some mistake.

That year, my family enjoyed a peaceful Lunar New Year holiday. We continued using borrowed wheat, and on New Year's Eve and New Year's Day, Father let me and my siblings fill our bellies with two delicious servings of dumplings. That year Father smoked more tobacco than on any other New Year's Day—almost as though he were trying to inhale an entire lifetime of smoke during that single festival.

It was that same year that I began to develop my secret plan—perhaps preemptively paving a road for a later escape from this life and this world, perhaps as an attempt to shore up my strength for a future struggle, or perhaps it was an act of unconsciously setting a future trap for Father and our family. In any event, I came up with the idea of leaving home, and resolved that if I didn't have other options in a few years, I would run off and join the army.

6. WARFARE

In reality, what I developed was not so much a plan as a selfish desire. A thought can always be rebutted or can change on its own, while a belief can only be suppressed. During my first winter after finishing middle school, as soon as I turned sixteen, I calmly went to enroll in the military. Upon returning home, I was met by Mother, who had tears streaming down her face, and Father, who offered some light but firm words of persuasion.

He said, "Lianke, why don't you stay in school for a few more years? In this life, education is fundamental. Even if you are fated to become an official or a king, if you don't have any understanding of culture, then you won't have a stable foundation on which to sit."

This was my father. He was tall and thin, and it seemed as though his face was perpetually the color of yellow soil. He could read only a few characters but always intervened in his children's labor, and every word he uttered invariably contained the sort of truth that rural peasants achieve only through a process of repeated practice.

In accordance with Father's instructions, I enrolled in high school. In accordance with the arrangement of fate, however, before graduating I proceeded to work for two years in the Xinxiang cement factory, where I would take my entire monthly salary, meager as it might have been, and send all of it (except for what I needed for food) home to my family—so that Father could repay the debts he had incurred to our neighbors, friends, and relatives while trying to treat Eldest Sister's illness. Thinking back now, I realize the extent to which my family must have relied on my monthly remittances, which must have functioned as a figurative paddle allowing our family's boat to ford the river of time. At the very least, the money I sent must have significantly lessened my father's burden as the head of household. However, when I was twenty and realized I wouldn't be able to pass the university entrance exams, I learned that one of Father's friends could arrange for me to join the army, and I knew that if I passed up this opportunity I might never be able to leave that arduous plot of land. So I went up to Father's bed in the middle of the night and said:

"Father, I want to join the army."

The room became extremely quiet. The light bulb hanging from the middle of the ceiling, which had burned out many years earlier, was enveloped in cobwebs, and the oil lamp was still the home's most important resident. The lamplight was the color of yellow earth, and as it shone on people's faces it gave them a sickly pallor. After I finished speaking, Mother sat up in bed and stared at me as though feeling that the house was about to collapse. She had a look of astonishment, which quickly shifted to an expression of unnamable anxiety. I initially thought Mother was about to say something to block the dream of leaving home that I had long been cherishing, but in the end she remained silent and instead slowly shifted her gaze to Father. As she did so, I heard the sound of boulders rolling down from the mountaintops onto the fields below and saw Father's sallow face staring up at me. Apart from the furrows on his forehead appearing deeper than usual, the rest of his face—his eyes, nose, and the corners of his mouth, which usually trembled from agitation—did not appear any different.

Over the last few years, I didn't know whether it was that Father's condition had improved or that Eldest Sister's had deteriorated, making Father appear better by comparison. Father sat at the head of the bed, wrapped in his blanket, with an unusually peaceful look on his face. He reacted to my announcement that I wanted to join the army as though I had informed him that I wanted to go to the market or to my uncle's or aunt's house for few days. He looked at me calmly and replied, "Go ahead. What would your prospects be if you stayed home?"

Thinking back, I realize Father was solemnly granting me permission. It was as if he were finally allowing me a response after having carefully considered my prospects for centuries. It was as if, in order to be able to grant his permission, he had been waiting for this request for a hundred years, as if he had been waiting until he was completely exhausted—which is why he now replied so calmly, perhaps even a bit impatiently.

Therefore, I resolutely went to join the army.

However, it wasn't so much that I was leaving to join the army but rather that I was escaping from the land. And it wasn't so much that I was escaping from the land but rather that I was betraying my family. And it wasn't so much that I was betraying my family but rather that I was giving up the responsibilities and obligations that a son should have for his father and his family. I was twenty years old and already had a strong pair of shoulders. Not only could I heft a 180-*jin* carrying pole, I could support all the tragedy that Father had previously been shouldering. But after Father granted me the strength to resist what seemed like my fate, I used this strength to rush away in a direction that my parents and my family did not want. After my physical and political exams, and relying on someone's recommendation, I finally received the notification that I had been appointed to the army.

I proceeded to put on a military uniform, which marked a crucial new moment in my life.

I left home on a cold winter morning, and the last thing that Father said to me was, "Lianke, don't worry. The sky won't collapse after you leave."

But not long after I left, it did.

On February 17, 1979, the southern border war known in China as the Sino-Vietnamese Self-Defensive Counterattack erupted. At the time, the Chinese military had not engaged in a conflict for twenty or thirty years, not since the Sino-Indian War, and consequently an atmosphere of peace had developed over the heads of China's population of one billion people. So, for both the army and the common people, the declaration of war seemed to come out of the blue. Naturally, a brownish-purple fear and blood-soaked anxiety descended, which can't even be imagined. To tell the truth, I wasn't an extraordinary officer, or even a particularly good soldier. I would never be able to yearn for war, and I was even less interested in making the sorts of great contributions and performing the kinds of important tasks that were expected from a soldier. This is an insight, an unforgettable spiritual awakening that I derived from a quarter century's service in the army.

Actually, I was extraordinarily fortunate—because a month after war broke out, I went to participate in a writers' workshop in the former Wuhan military region, and as I was passing through Zhengzhou on my way back, I was able to take a detour through my hometown. At sunset, when spring had just arrived and winter had not entirely passed, under the thin layer of sunlight, the bitter chill was thick and heavy. I trod over the rays of the setting sun as I came to the village and entered my house. When I arrived, Mother was stirring a bowl of soup paste. I shouted out to her, whereupon she looked up at me, stunned. The bowl froze for a moment in her hand, then fell to the ground and shattered into countless pieces, and the snow-white flour paste spilled out.

Upon returning home that day I saw my gray-haired first aunt, third aunt, and fourth aunt hurrying out of the room. Eldest Sister and Second Sister also came out, with tears in their eyes, as all our neighbors rushed over to our house. There wasn't anyone whose eyes stayed dry when they saw me, and there wasn't anyone whose face wasn't filled with joy and excitement at my unexpected return. Even when Mother had seen me, her face had lit up with surprise, beneath which was an unmistakable look of concern at my unexpected arrival.

My father was the last to emerge from our rear courtyard. He walked slowly, as though he were an old man. Although at that time he was still only fifty-two years old, his back was already hunched, and his face, which had previously been thin, now appeared so gaunt that it seemed to consist of only skin and bone. I couldn't understand how Father could have aged so much over the two months I was gone. His hair, which had been jet black, was now as white as snow. And every time he took a few steps, he would need to stop to catch his breath, as if he never had enough air. It was only then that I realized that in the month since the Sino-Vietnamese War had broken out, all of my family's relatives—more than thirty people in all—had moved into our home so that they could easily be kept up-to-date regarding my situation. Everyone was sleeping on the cold, hard floor, and all were eating the same basic fare from the communal pot. While eating, they would listen to the radio broadcasts for news about the front, and every day they would take turns going to the post office to see if there were any letters from me. They would also secretly go to the temple and burn incense in front of all sorts of gods and deities, praying for my safe return. As for Father, he was so worried about me on account of the war—compounded by the tumult of having so many relatives suddenly staying in his house—that he found himself unable to sleep at night. He would get out of bed every night and go to an empty area in the rear courtyard, where he would pace back and forth while staring out into the cold night. As the war dragged on for more than a month, Father had paced back and forth in the cold courtyard for more than thirty nights. For thirty long nights, the courtyard's damp earth was packed hard by his steps, and the grass sprouts that were struggling to emerge and meet the spring were ground back into the earth. In the end, the chronic asthma that had plagued him for years—and which had only gradually started to improve a bit—erupted again and was even more severe than before.

It turned out that this recurrence of Father's illness was the immediate cause of his death. If I hadn't seen this with my own eyes, I would never have been able to appreciate what an enormous effect the war could have on ordinary people. I would never have been able to appreciate how a father whose son had joined the army could become so worried about his son and the war.

During the two decades since Father's death, I've fantasized countless times about him walking alone in the quiet night under those three tung trees and one toon tree in our family's rear courtyard. The night was so cold, and the stars in the sky were so faint, and he, in order to avoid disturbing others, would have been treading very softly. What would he have been saying to the ground under his feet, which had been peaceful for thousands of years? What sort of feelings might he have had for this land? What would the grass sprouts—which had spent an entire winter waiting for the opportunity to emerge from the earth—have said to my father about my having left the land and ended up in a war? During those two months, the leaves of the tung trees didn't turn green, but the megaphone-shaped red flowers had already begun blooming recklessly. And the faint red sound of flowers blooming in the quiet sky—is this not the silent murmuring of my illiterate father, a true peasant, facing the endless night? Needless to say, in the cold, dark night, Father walked until he was exhausted, and when his asthma forced him to stop and rest, he would stand still and gaze up at the vast sky, hoping against hope to hear the faint sound of gunfire from the southern front, hoping to feel some tremors from that region in eastern Henan where his son's battalion was engaged in war. What was he thinking? And if he was asking even the simplest of questions, what might they be?

Whenever Mother woke up and saw that Father's bed was empty, she would go into the rear courtyard to look for him. Sometimes she would join him, pacing back and forth with him, and other times she would stand and watch as he paced and gazed up at the vast, silent sky. What would they discuss with one another? What were their deepest, most direct, and simplest thoughts about the war, about their son, and what were their views on life, fate, and humanity's existence in the world?

7. FATE

Others may have deep reflections on life and fate, but to tell the truth my own thoughts are very superficial. Because I missed Father, I would often wonder about this. These foolish thoughts would resemble what used to be called "pantomime," and what people today call playing a part or putting on a show. I couldn't help but think about these things, though at the same time I found myself unable to come up with a deeper, more novel understanding of fate. Like a student unable to explain the meaning of something, I kept returning to these foolish reflections the way tree leaves fall in autumn year after year. So I always treated my reflections as though they were the height of vanity.

I repeatedly speculated that fate is not directly causal, and in fact may not even contain any causality at all. Instead, it is an existential absolute and also a complete contingency. To be more precise, fate is a causal relation embedded within a broader contingency, and also an unexpected contingency that is contained within causality itself. It is causality outside of causality, the development of contingency outside of causality. When people are hungry, they eat, and if they have no food, they must endure hunger—this is not fate but simply reality. It snows in winter, and people who don't have fire or clothing may freeze to death. This is also not fate, but rather an explanation of mortal causality. However, if you originally plan to head east, but for some reason decide instead to head west, and then fall into a pit and break your leg, ending up crippled and unable to find a wife, have children, and establish a family—this perhaps might have something to do with fate. Similarly, if you are walking along the base of a mountain, holding your newly issued marriage certificate and singing happily, delighted that the next day you'll be able to move into your newlywed home, when suddenly an enormous stone rolls down the mountain and crushes your head, causing you to bid farewell to this world as your bright red marriage certificate falls to the ground—this too would be fate. This would be fate intervening in life. It is possible to cite countless similar examples, such as a tragic ending caused by a lightning strike on a sunny day, or the way a professor's idle joke might land him in prison. Or if a beggar suddenly stumbles across a vast fortune, but just as he is about to see his dreams come true, a cold knife suddenly comes down onto his head. Would it be accurate to say that life is the extension of happiness or suffering, while fate is a new beginning after the end of happiness or suffering? Life is a vertical progression, while fate is a horizontal change. Life is a blue-green lake, while fate is an endless, mysterious ocean. Or we might say that life is grass under the sun and rain, while fate is a scythe blade or a cow's teeth; life is ants tirelessly proceeding forward, while fate is a huge foot suddenly coming down out of nowhere; life is corn undergoing pollination and silking, while fate is a sudden downpour in the middle of this process. What else is there to say? We could add that if life is a process, then fate is an ending, or perhaps it is both an end and a new beginning; and if life is the dialogue and performance onstage, then fate is the closing of the curtain on one performance and its opening on the beginning of another. If you can say that life relies on fate in order to change, then fate doesn't necessarily rely on life in order to develop, because it develops on its own. In sum, life is a foundation, while fate is a process of sublimation or degradation that may or may not be related to this foundation. If life is accumulation, then fate is an extension or mutation that may or may not be related to this accumulation. If life has a measurable depth, then fate is a bottomless pit. If life has both tragedies and comedies, then fate is simply a tragedy. To put this another way, if life is happiness, then fate is tears; and if life is tears, then fate is soft sobbing. If life is soft sobbing, then fate is a process of tearlessly howling at the sky, and if life is a process of howling at the sky, then fate is dying before one can even begin howling.

In a word, fate is the prelude or the coda to the unpredictable tragedies that occur in life. It is the act of grinding one's feet into the ground in penitence and helplessness.

8. SIN

In the end, it was during wartime that my father fell, but it was because I wanted to join the army that he fell ill in the first place. His asthma quickly developed into pneumonia. He was still healthy enough over the summer, but winter was an absolute disaster: he coughed all day long, and spat up so much phlegm that for more than half a month he was barely able to sleep. It was as if his illness couldn't be blamed on the military conflict on the southern front and instead could be attributed only to his life and fate.

What is war? War's morphological essence is disaster, and disaster is a land mine sitting on flat ground or a thunderbolt on a clear day. How can ordinary people possibly anticipate this sort of disaster? To tell the truth, had I known what awaited me on my military path, I don't think I would have been so insistent on leaving the land and joining the army. I doubt I would have, without hesitation, handed over to my father all the burdens that a son should normally have shouldered. Indeed, in that scenario, all the remaining questions would have been very clear—I could easily have chosen not to enlist in the army, just as I could easily have decided to stay behind to work the land, as thousands of others from my generation had done. So why did I go? If I hadn't, would Father still have suffered a relapse after having been all but cured of his illness for several years? And if he hadn't suffered a relapse, would he still have departed from this bitter world at the age of only fifty-eight? With respect to Father's illness and death, if it can be said that his fate was responsible for creating the kind of life he led, then who was responsible for his fate? What role did I myself play in his sad and miserable fate? What effect did I have?

During Father's illness and the initial months and years after his passing, I rarely considered these obvious questions. In reality, I didn't even dare consider them, because I was afraid that if I did, the responsibility and fault I would have to bear would then be laid out clearly before me. Just as some students never look at the corrections teachers make on their homework, I always avoided these most direct and simple of questions, in order to feel I could make up for them with "filial" conduct—though in reality I was simply covering up mistakes and sins for which I would never be able to atone, for as long as I lived.

Early on, more than a decade before my elder brother installed a phone line in our house, I made a point of writing home twice a month to report that everything was okay. Now communication technologies are more advanced, and I can call my mother long-distance every two or three days just to chat about idle matters, to maintain a line of contact that appears casual but in fact is an absolute necessity. It has now been three decades that I've been living away from my hometown and from our land, but every Lunar New Year I make every effort to return home for the holidays. Even when I was serving as a soldier or just after I had been promoted to cadre, I would still, like clockwork, come up with some excuse in order to find a way to return home and observe the traditional New Year's Eve celebrations with Mother. On the rare occasions when there was really no way for me to return home for New Year's Day, I would still find a way to return for day five or day fifteen. Initially, one task I would perform every time I returned home would be to take the pile of letters and notes I had written to Mother over the course of the preceding year and either rip them up or burn them, so that no one would be able to find in them some secret content behind the words' actual meaning. Back when I was receiving a subsidy of six or eight yuan a month, I would send some money home once every three months, and after I was promoted to cadre and given a monthly salary, I would set aside what I needed for food and a small amount of spending money, and I would send home all the rest to help pay for Father's medicine and treatment.

In principle, God is always watching us, and even when he appears to be sleeping, he may always have one of his eyes open. God was apparently afraid that my family's difficulties would accumulate until they exploded. Given that disaster always signals both an end and a new beginning, God permitted my eldest sister, after she had endured seventeen years of agony, to find that her condition had finally begun to improve, and then God let all of us siblings once again begin frantically running around—as though competing in a relay race—to buy Father medicine and take him to the doctor.

At that point, Elder Brother was already working as a temporary mailman and earning twenty-six yuan and eighty cents a month, and every day he would bike several dozen *li* along mountain roads to deliver letters and newspapers. In the canteen, he would always eat the cheapest food, and sometimes he would skip lunch altogether and eat only breakfast and dinner, so that he could send home the money he saved. Because of her health, Eldest Sister was given a job teaching in an elementary school, and every month was issued twelve yuan in salary. Meanwhile, in addition to farming and helping Mother cook and wash clothes, Second Sister continued hauling sand and stones, while also performing manual labor for the construction team. And finally there was Mother—our beloved mother. Mother had to endure more material and psychological pressure than any of us siblings, and she would continually work the land, raise the pigs and chickens, and attend to each of our marriage arrangements, while at the same time organizing Father's medicine each day. You could say that Father's life was almost entirely reliant on his medicine and on Mother's care, and therefore every day Mother would silently endure and sustain him. She made a rough assessment and determined that during that period in the early eighties, any day that Father had five or six yuan to spend on medicine, his life would be significantly improved, but if he didn't, he would have difficulty enduring the misery that I had brought him as a result of my departure. But at that time it was extremely difficult to get five or six yuan a day. On top of that, the family also had to think about Eldest Sister's and Elder Brother's wedding arrangements and about fixing the roof when it leaked, together with daily expenses for items like salt and coal. In this respect, our family's predicament during that period was much worse than it had been at the height of Eldest Sister's illness.

In the winter of 1982, Father's illness took a turn for the worse. At that point, I had already been serving in the army for four years, where I worked as an administrator in the division library. When my family's poverty hit rock bottom, my parents thought of me and the military hospital to which I had a connection. On the one hand, this was because the military hospital carried a mysterious air; on the other hand, it was because they thought that if they could access the military hospital, they could avoid paying medical fees for my father. So I requested a leave of absence and returned home to fetch my parents. I remember that it was Elder Brother who escorted me and my parents to the train that would take us from Luoyang to Shangqiu, more than a hundred *li* away. As the train began to leave the station, Elder Brother bid me farewell through the window, saying, "I'm afraid that Father's illness won't improve, but you must definitely find a way for him to spend a few days in the hospital, because he'll be more comfortable there than at home." He added, "As long as Father can stay in the hospital and receive some treatment, some of our guilt will be assuaged after he passes away." It was, in fact, with a somewhat lightened heart that I had gone to fetch Father, but after we got off the train before nightfall and proceeded toward the entrance to the division hospital, Father called me over and said, "Ever since I first fell ill, I've never had a chance to stay in a hospital. This army hospital is very proper, with good equipment and technology. We've now traveled several hundred *li* by car and train, but we don't have any money to pay a bill. If they don't admit me, you should kneel down and beg the doctors, and I'll do the same."

I immediately burst into tears.

I knew that the equipment and technology of the division hospital weren't as good as those of the rural county hospital, and I knew that even though Father's illness was not necessarily terminal, his symptoms were nevertheless very difficult to cure. The main reason we were taking him to the military hospital more than one hundred *li* away was that there was a possibility that he could be treated there for free. At that moment, I wiped away my tears and said, "Father, we've already made arrangements with the hospital, and they'll definitely admit you once we arrive." Then, I took the letter of introduction that read, "Please admit this patient," which the cultural division section chief had prepared for us, and showed it to him. Father gazed at that letter, and a look of excitement appeared on his face. With a smile, he said, "I had never expected I'd be admitted to a hospital. Perhaps my illness will be cured there, and if so, then your having joined the army will have been worth it."

Needless to say, Father arrived at the hospital with great hopes that he might be cured. During the first two weeks, because the hospital was kept warm and he was in good spirits, his illness did appear to improve somewhat. Those two weeks were the most reassuring period of my life, because it was the only time that I looked after Father with complete filial devotion. Every day, I would head into the wind and walk four or five *li* to take him his food, while humming opera lines or melodies. Once, when I took Father his dinner, he and Mother were not in the hospital room, and instead I found them attending an open-air film screening, where they were standing outside in the cold but completely absorbed by the movie. When I saw this, my heart filled with happiness, because I thought Father's condition had finally improved. I quickly called up my siblings to tell them about this development. Father also felt that his illness was improving, and when he returned to his room after the movie, he observed happily that it had been years since he had seen a movie, and that he had coughed only a few times while watching outside on a cold winter night.

However, three days later there was a snowstorm, and the temperature dropped abruptly. By this point Father had stopped taking his medicine and getting his shots, and consequently he found himself barely able to breathe. Even after he received shots and intravenous transfusions, his breathing became increasingly difficult, to the point that he ultimately couldn't go without an oxygen tank. The doctors encouraged us to check out of the hospital, afraid that Father might suddenly stop breathing while lying there. Father himself said, "If I don't hurry home, I'm afraid I'll 'age out' while away from home." This marked the end of my short-lived period of bedside piety.

Around that time, it had become popular in the countryside for projectionists to visit people's houses to screen a movie with a sixteen-millimeter projector, each screening costing ten yuan. A projectionist visited our village with the film *Shaolin Temple*, and we proposed that he come to our house so that Father, while lying in bed, could watch this film in which people climb walls and fly over rooftops. Father also very much liked the idea, but when the projectionist arrived, Mother said, "Forget it. With these ten yuan, we can help your father survive another day." My siblings and I looked at each other in surprise, but had no choice but to send the projectionist away. This moment marked a lack of filiality that I would always regret, and whenever I remembered it, I felt an acute ache in my heart. When we took Father to his grave, my sisters sobbed, bemoaning the fact that when Father was alive he hadn't been able to watch a movie he wanted to see (even if it was just a single screening). Then they cursed themselves for their "lack of filiality." I saw that when Elder Brother, who by this point had already stopped crying, heard this, his face immediately turned pale and twisted, and his tears once again began pouring forth like rain. I realized that my siblings perhaps felt even guiltier about this incident than I did.

Another source of acute guilt, one that I bore alone, meanwhile, was that when I got married on National Day in 1984, I didn't buy my wife a present or a new set of clothes. Instead, I borrowed 120 yuan to pay for the wedding—which for her would be a once-in-a-lifetime event. My wife, however, expressed no complaints about this. The first time I took her home to meet my parents, our visit happened to coincide with a sudden autumn downpour, as a result of which, Father's illness took a turn for the worse, making it necessary for my family to run around frantically calling on doctors, buying medicine, providing oxygen, and boiling soup. No one dared step away from Father's sickbed. As soon as that night's storm passed, the sky began to clear. The stars overhead appeared cold and sparse, while inside the room was chilled and filled with our concern for Father. Everyone walked slowly and spoke softly, as though afraid of interrupting Father's weak breathing and frightening away his fragile soul. When Father's condition finally improved a little, the doctor called Mother and me into another room and said that Father's body was simply too weak. The doctor said that Father would need some expensive medicines, and asked, "Does your family have any money?" Mother shook her head, as I buried my head in my chest and for a long time didn't say a word. Seeing this, the doctor sighed, then said, in a very professional tone, "As long as Second Uncle (which is to say, my father) is alive, I'm afraid your family won't be able to enjoy a good life; and if your family is going to have a good life, then that means that Second Uncle only has a few days to live."

I don't know whether this rural doctor, who had struggled valiantly during Father's illness, was offering a judgment on Father's life, or was instead offering an assessment of our household's prospects for survival, given that ours was a very ordinary rural family.

When he finished, he and Mother went over to Father's bed, but I, for some reason, continued standing there without moving. My head was buzzing, and it was as if the doctor's words had given me a very inauspicious premonition. After standing there for I don't know how long, I finally walked out of the house and proceeded to go into the winter night, gazing up at the ice-cold sky. I felt as though there were an explosion inside my skull. I have no idea why, but suddenly I heard the doctor's remark echo again in my head: *As long as Second Uncle is alive, I'm afraid your family won't be able to enjoy a good life . . .* If I had repeated the doctor's remark in its entirety, that would have been okay, and if I had considered this remark's full connotations, that would also have been okay. But at that moment, that single phrase continued to echo in my head, becoming wedged in my brain like a shard of ice. It was not the phrase itself that became stuck in my head but rather its implications: *As long as Father is alive, our family (or perhaps just me) won't be able to enjoy a good life.* That is to say, this phrase inadvertently expressed my anticipation of Father's death and my frustration with the burden brought about by his chronic illness. At the time, when I abruptly realized that the doctor's phrase was still echoing in my head, it seemed to imply: *I hope that Father will die soon* and *I want to use Father's death in order to regain our family's (or just my) happy lives.* When I realized this, a cold tremor engulfed my body, jolting me from my head to my toes. It was as though I were afraid that Father would be able to hear my thoughts and that Mother and my elder siblings would emerge and see the despicable sin hidden deep in my heart. I rushed from the main courtyard to hide in the smaller courtyard at the back of the house.

The latter courtyard—where Father had paced back and forth every night after I joined the army, as a result of which he had repeatedly fallen ill—was dark and damp, quiet and mysterious. The shadows of the tung and toon trees, which by then had already lost most of their leaves, swayed back and forth, and the trees' remaining leaves rustled in the breeze. The thick smell of moisture and decay rolled around, and as I stood in the center of the courtyard in the middle of the dark night, I felt as though I had been pushed into the center of an endless ocean or mountain range, and my entire body was struck with great solitude and bitter cold. I began punishing myself for my sinful thoughts by repeatedly slapping my own ears, then pinching my face, my torso, and my legs . . .

But by this point it was already too late. It was as though God wanted me to give my soul an eternal punishment and had used all the abilities and experience he commanded. Two months later, God finally summoned Father, forcing him to depart from Mother, from his children, and from his nieces and nephews who treated him as though they were also part of his immediate family, as if they were his daughters and sons. He made Father depart from this countryside and this world that Father had loved so bitterly.

9. CLEARING DEBTS

Now I am finally able to calculate the debt I owe Father.

I can finally clear my conscience. First, though, I should note that I never spent those ten yuan that we were originally going to use to let Father watch *Shaolin Temple*. At the time, I definitely had some money, and I remember that after I returned to my barracks, I still had seventeen yuan in my pocket. That is to say, I definitely could have afforded ten yuan for the film screening, to let Father watch with his own eyes that legendary practice of "climbing walls and flying over rooftops" he had dreamed of his entire life. Why had I been unwilling to spend those ten yuan? Of course, it was simply stinginess and frugality, combined with the general financial pressures under which we were operating at the time. But was there a more important reason? Was it that I had never developed a sense of consideration and filial love for Father when I was young? Was it related to how, when I was three or five years old—or even later, when I was in my teens—and whenever Father returned from working in the mountains or in the fields, he would give me a handful of red dates or some other wild fruits that he couldn't bring himself to eat, and I would always squat down in a corner and devour them all by myself, and I didn't think to share some with him? Thinking back, I realize that there is something to this. Before I joined the army, I had never bought Father anything to eat or to wear. In fact, when I returned from working in the fields, I never even brought him a fresh ear of corn. But if it wasn't that I was selfish and loveless, then why wasn't I able to spend just ten yuan on Father's behalf when I had the opportunity to do so? People are often like this—understanding things only after it is too late, and becoming generous and selfless only when those qualities are no longer needed. Only when they are pushed do they become generous and impassioned. Without a doubt, I was indeed that kind of person. I was the kind of person who, when the weather turns cold, always dresses himself first and when it warms up, thinks first of positioning himself in the shade. This kind of person always prioritizes himself over others, including his own father. This kind of person is quiet and self-effacing when helping himself but is loud and triumphant when helping others. Furthermore, this loud and triumphant behavior helps conceal such a person's practice of prioritizing himself. If I think carefully, I realize that I was in fact like this. When I didn't rent that film for Father, the ostensible reason was the expense—but if it had been the case that I didn't have enough money at the time, then why did I still have nearly twenty yuan when I returned to my barracks? If it was in fact true that, from the time I was young, I had really loved Father more than I loved myself, and I had in fact been the kind of person who

placed the highest importance on attending to Father's food, clothing, and general happiness, then how could I possibly have decided
not to organize that movie screening? Why was it only after Father's
death that I finally began to feel regret over this incident? Did this
not amount to wearing a padded jacket over one's own ice-cold
love? Did it not amount to warming up one's love and goodness,
and publicizing it by placing it in an opening in the shade, so that
everyone can see it? To this day, I continue to believe that one can
always hold back when dealing with acquaintances, but one cannot
do so when it comes to dealing with one's own parents or with anyone connected by blood, such as one's siblings or children—even if
it entails the risk of shedding of blood or even of death. However, I
did not abide by this principle.

The second debt I incurred is that I insisted on enlisting in
the army and fleeing our land, and even if others may have believed
that doing so was perfectly reasonable, actually I radically altered
my father's fate, making him suffer a relapse that, six years later, led
to his death and his departure from this world that he loved. This is
something I will always regret and something I will continually try
to explain away by appealing to issues of survival, future prospects,
and struggle. It is true that I was continually trying to explain this
away, because I couldn't bear to face up to the fact that my actions
had been a key factor leading to Father's premature death.

It is also on account of my inability to face these realities that
my unconscious came up with that sinful thought: *As long as Father
is alive, my family (which is to say, I) won't be able to have a good life.*
This is the third debt I owe Father, and it is a sin of which I'll never
be able to absolve myself—to the point that it is the best basis for
God to exercise his power and summon Father. But did Father know
all this when he was alive? He was a step ahead of us in experiencing life and death. What was he thinking before his death? People

experience being alive, but they can only speculate about what it means to be dead. Is death a punishment for life, or is it instead a form of transcendence? Perhaps it is both punishment *and* transcendence? Or perhaps it is neither punishment nor transcendence and instead is simply an ending. Some people enjoy wealth and luxury while they are alive and therefore are unwilling to part with this life and are afraid to die. For others, however, it is precisely because they have enjoyed wealth and luxury that they are therefore able to greet death with a smile, viewing it as a form of transcendence. Meanwhile, there are also some people who, because their life is hard and miserable, view death as a rebirth and can truly treat death as a form of transcendence, something to which they can look forward. But my father belonged to none of these categories. He treasured life precisely because he had experienced hardship, and it was because he had experienced hardship that he was able to appreciate life's significance and its subtle pleasures. In the spring, he would put on his face mask and sit outside in the courtyard, resisting the final traces of winter's chill, and watch people walk by. In this way, he was able to recover his memory of the countryside, which he had nearly forgotten during his illness. In the summer, he would stroll around the entryway to his house, to the entrance to the village, and through the fields, watching the growing crops and the lazy dogs and the chickens—and in this way he would gain a new appreciation for the world's existence and for the warmth of existence. In autumn, he would sit somewhere sheltered from the wind, keeping an eye on the grain Mother had sifted and washed, and watch the geese fly south. He would slowly remember the fields he had sowed, the crops he had harvested, and his life and experiences as a peasant. And during the cold winters of his life, when the north wind would blow and his breathing would become more difficult, he would surround himself with his nieces and nephews to form a human furnace, or else he would lie in bed wrapped in the quilt that Mother and Elder Sister had made him, holding that bowl of Chinese medicine that my sensible wife had prepared for him. He would watch his grandson Fangfang and granddaughter Yuanyuan play, enjoying the happiness that only being with relatives and close family can bring. Why wouldn't he be reluctant to leave this world? The footpath through the fields still demanded that he stroll down it; his neighbors' arguments still called for him to go and mediate; and the routine challenges his children encountered after they got married and established their own families still required that he advise and arbitrate. As for his grandchildren, grandnephews, and grandnieces, he still needed to take them out to the entryway and watch them play.

Father really had no reason to leave this world prematurely or to be reluctant to depart it. Given that he was a peasant, as long as he could live in this world and in the same space with his family, suffering would be a kind of enjoyment or even a kind of pleasure. Father clearly understood this, and therefore viewed death as God's way of punishing him, but he had no idea what—after having diligently done his duty his entire life—he could possibly have done to deserve this punishment. When he realized he was about to leave this world, his eyes filled with tears of frustration, until finally he entreated me and my elder brother, saying, "Quick, go call the doctor. See if he can find a way to help me live a few more days . . ." Meanwhile, his dying words concerned Mother's care. He said to her, "Our two sons and their wives live and work in the city. They are city folk. But we are peasants and are used to living in the countryside. After I die, you should continue to lead your own life in the countryside, because if you move to the city you may find it hard to adjust . . ."

The last thing Father said to me was, "You're back? Quick, go get something to eat." This was in 1984, at noon on the thirteenth day of the eleventh lunar month. The previous day I had received a telegram saying that Father was terminally ill, so I had hurried home immediately with my wife, arriving at noon on the thirteenth. I stood in front of Father's bed, and as he gazed at me one final time, his eyes overflowing with tears, he uttered his final words to me—which were also his final words in this world. It was as if he had been waiting for me to return in order to make this pronouncement. It was as if he weren't willing to be in the same space with a son like me, and therefore not long after he said these words, his breathing became labored, and the expression of misery and sorrow on his face turned a greenish purple. At this point, I climbed onto his bed and cradled his head to my chest, as I tried to help the doctor save him. But just as Father's head came to rest on my chest, and just as my hand grasped his, he stopped breathing. He jerked his head to the side, and it slipped off my chest. Then he released his grip on my hand, and two streaks of tears flowed down his cheeks. If Father didn't treasure this world, would he have shed those desolate tears during the final moments of his life? But if he did treasure this world, then why was he willing to leave it? And before leaving, why did he turn his head away from my chest, and why did he release his grip on my hand? Wasn't all of this because in leaning against me he heard an echo of that evil thought in my heart: *Will we not be able to enjoy life until after Father dies?*

If we compare people to animals, we can observe that there is a kind of insect that, after it gives birth, uses its own flesh and blood as nourishment for its young, to help raise them to adulthood. What meaning of life is expressed in this scenario? There is also a kind of wolf with a light-colored coat that, when it has food, will share its food with its parents, but if it goes for seven days without being able to find food, it will kill its elderly parents and devour them. When this happens, the wolf's parents watch silently as their own offspring bites them until they are covered in blood. Am I not just like the insect or the wolf that consumes its own parents? And even if I'm not, is it not still true that I harbor evil tendencies? From an everyday occurrence like the time I declined to spend ten yuan to screen a movie for my father, to my insistence on fleeing our land to join the army, not to mention my willingness to keep evil thoughts in my heart . . . What kind of son am I? Is it that after undergoing this process of repentance and purification, when facing Father I'll be able to confront the final questions of my conscience? I reflected on the fact that what I owed Father was not money or goods but rather life and fate. First Uncle would be eighty-three when he died, Third Uncle almost eighty, and Fourth Uncle, who passed away just last year, sixty-nine. If my father had survived long enough to reach the average of their respective ages, he would have lived to at least seventy-five or seventy-six. Instead, he was only fifty-eight when he died. How will I ever repay this debt of eighteen years by which Father's life was cut short? In our village, there was someone who suffered from the same illness as Father but lived to the age of seventy-six. If I hadn't triggered Father's relapse, might he perhaps have reached the age of seventy-six, or even eighty?

10. SETTLING ACCOUNTS

The willow saplings over Father's grave have already grown into tall trees, and many things have changed over the course of the three decades since his death. The only thing that hasn't changed is Father's peaceful rest, and the guilt and longing I feel on his behalf. Needless to say, as Father lies in the Yan clan's ancestral grave, he is waiting for his son's final return. When we were burying Father, First Uncle marked the site of Father's grave and then marked three more squares for the locations of the future graves of the other three men of his generation. Finally, he gestured to a plot below Father's grave, and said, "Eventually, Fa'ke (my elder brother) and Lianke will be buried here."

I know that in my family's ancestral grave there is a plot with my name on it. When my time comes, I'm confident that I'll work hard to be a filial son, in order to make up for my lack of filiality while Father was still alive.

Other than this, I don't have anything else to say.

CHAPTER 4

First Uncle's Family

1. A HISTORICAL FIGURE

Although First Uncle was without a doubt a peasant, in my mind he was a true historical figure. With respect to what he had survived in his life, he was a great, even exemplary, figure.

Every time I saw First Uncle, or remembered him after his death, I always had the same thought: if only he hadn't had to spend his entire life trying to survive, and if only he'd had an opportunity to join the revolutionary tide—like those revolutionaries who arrived at Yan'an at the end of the Long March—then with his decency and bravery, and with his deep understanding of life and survival, he definitely could have been forged into a division or corps commander.

If only he had learned how to read, his prospects would have been limitless.

I never considered what Father's prospects might have been, but I always thought it was truly a shame that First Uncle had had to spend his entire life on that tiny plot of land, where he worked day and night, raised a family, and finally succumbed to illness. It always seemed to me that this was a betrayal of his life and his character, of his talents and his tenacity.

2. KNITTED SOCKS

My strongest memory from my early childhood was from what must have been the early sixties. First Uncle had eight children—six boys and two girls—and together with First Uncle and his wife, that made ten people in all. China had just recovered from the so-called Three Years of Natural Disasters, in which millions of people starved to death, and their bones weren't even cold. In the cemetery the weeds had not yet had a chance to cover those freshly dug piles of yellow earth. When First Uncle began to experience hunger, he took his loom and began walking up and down all the streets and alleys of our mountain district. He would stop at every house, put down his carrying pole, wipe the sweat from his brow, and call out:

"Knitted socks . . ."

"Knitted wool socks . . ."

I don't know how First Uncle managed to successfully lead his wife and eight children through those Three Years of Natural Disasters. Later, the village elders would often relate how, during that period, they had to resort to eating dirt, and used axes and cleavers to strip bark from the trees to make a kind of broth. They related how, in the village, everyone's legs and face swelled up like plastic bladders full of water. They related how, in the mountains, the corpses of people who had died from hunger would lie in the open for days, growing rigid, as famished vultures circled overhead and periodically dove down and pecked at them.

By now, it has already been three years since First Uncle passed away, while First Aunt, who is now eighty years old, suffers from diabetes and dementia and consequently has become increasingly incoherent and taciturn. I regret that I never asked them about that three-year period while there was still time. I regret that I didn't ask them how they managed, with so many children, to survive those thousand days and nights when the country endured extreme famine. It occurs to me that what I missed was not only an important episode in the historical record but also an epic story in which the peasants of this great country resisted famine and death for the sake of life and love. But now virtually all I remember from that period is First Uncle's hoarse voice repeatedly calling through the mountains and villages:

"Knitted socks . . ."

"Knitted wool socks . . ."

First Uncle's loom consisted of a steel frame, numerous gears, a needle and mallet, and a hand crank; and all you had to do was arrange the machine-made yarn, twisting it together in an orderly fashion, and by turning the handle you could make all sorts of socks—large and small, long and short. Because that loom was foreign technology, and because it used machine-made yarn and not the handwoven kind that was traditionally used in the countryside, the loom was called a "foreign-sock machine" and the socks were called "foreign socks." Other things that were called "foreign" at the time included everyday items associated with foreigners, such as "foreign fire" (matches), "foreign nails" (steel nails), "foreign lime" (cement), "foreign axes" (pickaxes), and so forth. In each case, the modifier *foreign* added a connotation of quality and fashion, thereby lending the corresponding items a distinctive style and bearing. As a result, First Uncle's loom and the handicraft with which he made his foreign socks became known far and wide, and every winter he would take his carrying pole and travel deep into the two mountains to the east and west, weaving socks for peasants who ordinarily had to travel several dozen *li* just to buy some nails. As the end of the year approached, he'd return from the mountains and set up his loom at the front of his village, where he would knit foreign socks for neighbors and passersby.

Of course, First Uncle didn't charge anything when he knitted socks for his fellow villagers—nor did he ask for any other compensation. Instead, the only thing he accepted was the villagers' mutual support and care, since everyone in the countryside struggled together for survival. Only when he went on the road and knitted socks for strangers did he accept small amounts of money to help cover his household expenses.

I used to help First Uncle turn the crank for his loom. The crank was very loud and heavy, and each time I finished a pair of socks, my arm would feel as though it were about to fall off. First Uncle spent nearly a decade hoisting his carrying pole and turning that heavy crank, which represented the capital on which his children would rely for their survival. He would leave the village with his loom and his shoulder pole before dawn, and three or five days later he would return with them at dusk.

Each time First Uncle left the village, he would carry his loom on one end of his shoulder pole and his relatively light yarn and other provisions on the other. Because the weight was unevenly distributed, one side of the pole would need to be farther over his shoulder than the other. When he returned, the pole would be centered over his shoulders. By this point, his yarn already would have been used up and he already would have consumed all of his provisions. Instead, the sack in which he normally carried his yarn would be half-filled with corn and dried sweet potato, together with soybeans and green beans. This was compensation he received in return for knitting socks, and it constituted his family's sustenance and its very survival. However, at that time, my siblings, cousins, and I didn't pay much attention to the food and grain in First Uncle's sack; we were fixated instead on the things that he would be carrying in his coat pockets.

This was particularly true of me.

In spring and fall, First Uncle would always wear a black lined jacket with countless patches, and in the cold winter he would wear a padded jacket so old that its padding had already begun to decompose, and was poking out through holes in the fabric. However, the cloth sack that First Uncle carried on his shoulder pole would always be in good condition, and he would never let a single grain of food drop to the ground. His jacket pockets often looked as if they were about to rip open, but whenever he noticed this he would tell his eldest daughter to quickly sew them up for him. Anything else could be damaged or lost, but not those pockets. This is because every time First Uncle returned to the village after having been away for a few days, he would bring his children, nieces, and nephews some yummy snacks in his jacket pockets.

The snacks First Uncle brought back were often food and candy of a kind you can't find anymore. The food included hard, black crispy crackers, and there would be two kinds of candy: small candies individually wrapped in oiled paper and white candied beans. The candied beans were like today's soybeans, in that they were round and white, and in First Uncle's pockets they resembled a packet of pills. After First Uncle had spent three days on the road, we would start to look forward to his return and to the treats he would have in his pockets. After three days, in the period between sunset and nightfall, First Aunt would stand in the intersection in front of their house, holding her hand to her forehead as she gazed down the street, waiting for First Uncle's return.

On the third day, he wouldn't return.

On the fourth day, he wouldn't return.

On the fifth day, at around that same time, when the village was filled with the warm light of the setting sun, First Aunt would be in the village entrance waiting for First Uncle, but the first person to see First Uncle return usually was not First Aunt but rather one of us. We were so excited to receive the crackers and candy that we almost couldn't wait for First Uncle to arrive. Someone would shout, "First Uncle has returned . . ." and First Uncle would appear, hauling his shoulder pole and dragging himself forward. But upon entering the village and seeing his children and nieces and nephews waiting for him, he would quicken his pace, and his face would glow. As he proceeded toward us, we would run to greet him. We would crowd around him in the middle of the road, whereupon he would take a handful of crackers and candies from his pocket and distribute them into our small, dirty hands, as though planting beans in a field.

The other children and I would extend our hands to receive the snacks we had been waiting for. After First Uncle finished distributing the crackers and candies, we would savor them as though they were priceless treasures. First Uncle would then remove one of his shoes and sit on it, and then he would watch as we first ate the candy and then folded the wrappers into triangles and squares or else fashioned them into butterflies or dragonflies. We would blow or wave air at these paper objects, so they would fly around in the light of the setting sun. That was always the period when First Uncle was happiest and probably was also when he was most appreciative of life. He would sit in the village entrance—on the ground in the middle of a crowd of people—his face beaming with pleasure, and regardless of how dirty and exhausted he might be, he couldn't conceal his excitement.

First Uncle loved life, his children, and his cohort of nephews and nieces. Every time he distributed the candies and crisp black crackers, he would always first gaze down at the children crowded around him. He would always give everyone exactly the same amount—one piece of candy, two candied beans, and one cracker—but he would always give careful consideration to which children he distributed them to first. That is to say, he would always start with his nephews and nieces who lived farthest away, and his neighbor's children, and then would proceed to his nieces and nephews who lived closer by—including me and my siblings, and my other uncle's children. Finally, he would turn to his own children. Because he would invariably run out of snacks before he got to everyone, his own children would have to watch as the rest of us ate, played, and folded the colorful candy wrappers into the birds and insects we would then fly through the air.

Later, whenever First Uncle returned from one of his trips, I stopped crowding around to receive the candies, because I had observed this pattern: First Uncle would often run out of candy, and if someone had to do without, it was always his own children. So whenever he was distributing candy, I would wait with his children to see whether or not there was any candy left over at the end.

One time when First Uncle did in fact run out of snacks, I stood at the back with his own children, watching as everyone else threw the candy wrappers up in the air or made them into tiny kites. My eyes, for some reason, filled with tears out of a sense of injustice. First Uncle happened to see me, and he came over to pat my head and caress my face, as though he had just wronged me somehow. With a red face and a hoarse voice, he laughed, bitterly, and then said solemnly, "Next time I return, I'll buy some extra candy and will give you some first. I'll give you some before everyone else has a chance to eat."

3. FAVORITISM

That year, I started school.

Even after becoming a student, however, I still looked forward to when First Uncle, after having left the village to sell socks, would return with his pockets full of candy. During that time, I'm not sure whether he returned after three days or after five days, nor am I certain whether he returned to the village at sunset or before dusk.

I became busy with school and more and more often began missing the opportunity to enjoy First Uncle's candy.

I seemed to have forgotten how it was when First Uncle would come back every few days to give us candy. But one day, I was heading home after school, kicking at rocks on the side of the road and playing with some old marbles, when I suddenly saw a crowd of people standing in the middle of the road, and I saw too First Uncle's loom on the ground nearby. The loom was illuminated in the light of the setting sun, like a memorial tablet.

I rushed up to them.

As I approached, I timidly stood at the edge of the crowd. I remembered that I was already a student and therefore shouldn't compete with the children for the candies, which were probably in short supply. Instead, I stood quietly outside of that circle of outstretched hands. At that point, First Uncle saw me and the little book bag I was carrying. He broke through the ring of tiny hands and walked away from the circle of nephews and nieces and several of his own children who were even younger than me. He walked over to me and said, "You're in school now?"

I nodded.

First Uncle said, "You should study hard. Your uncle doesn't know how to read, and when he is out knitting socks, it's extremely difficult for him to even calculate how much change to give his customers."

As he was saying this, First Uncle took all the candies and crackers out of his pocket and stuffed them into my hand. Seeing that I couldn't hold them all, he removed my hat and filled it as well. Then he told me to take them home.

That time, I took away all the candy and crackers First Uncle had bought for his own children. The colorful snacks completely covered the bottom of my hat. As I walked away under the other children's jealous gazes, I didn't look back nor did I have any intention of giving a single piece of candy to anyone else. I knew First Uncle had given me the snacks because I had started school and had become a student—which meant that they all belonged to me. I wanted to savor them, the same way that now that I'm in my fifties, I savor my memories of First Uncle, who passed away three years ago. To this day, I still vividly recall the sweetness of those candies in a lifetime of endless bitterness.

4. ERUPTION

In raising one's children, one must always make sure that they have enough to eat, that they have warm clothes to wear, and that they receive some education. The most important thing, though, is to make sure that hunger won't hinder their development. These were the beliefs and aspirations of my father's generation.

Needless to say, First Uncle was no exception.

With a diameter of about one foot eight inches, the pot First Uncle's family used for cooking was probably the largest in the village. Because First Uncle had a lot of children, when cooking rice his family always added water until it reached the pot's rim. As a result, when it was necessary to "improve life" a bit—such as for a holiday or some other celebratory occasion—that wide-mouthed pot would appear small. For a holiday or celebratory occasion, a potful of rice simply wouldn't be enough. Instead, what we called improving life involved cooking a pot of noodle soup—or what my family called soup-paste noodles, which we made by putting corn dregs, hand-rolled noodles, green vegetables, and salt into a large pot and boiling them. Because we added extra noodles and greens, a little more oil, and might have also added some pieces of meat or fried pork dregs, we called this process improving life.

The food was quite good, but the pot inevitably appeared small. The children complained that they had already reached the bottom but hadn't yet had their fill. At this point, First Uncle would be sitting either on the doorstep of his family's house or on a stone at their front gate. Normally he would always eat two or three bowls, but on these occasions he would have only a bowl and a half before announcing that he was full. Clearly, he wanted to leave more food for us children.

And so it was that we grew up alternating between hunger and satiation. We all wore tattered clothing, and when we went to school we didn't have a backpack and instead carried our schoolbooks, sometimes in a small bag, tucked under our arm. When it rained, we didn't have rubber boots to wear, but we couldn't wear our cloth shoes, so we had no choice but to go out barefoot. Water red with blood would seep out from under our feet, as though spurting out of a tube, for it was common for us to have to walk barefoot over the shards of broken glass and ceramic embedded in the concrete.

With the arrival of winter's bitter cold, ice and snow closed off the mountain region of western Henan where we lived, and the weather became so frigid that even the air itself appeared icy. Everyone stayed home, huddled around the fire. First Uncle's family had many children—too many to fit around a single stove. It would have been too extravagant and wasteful to light two stoves, so First Uncle would step aside and let his children crowd around the stove for warmth.

Year after year, every time I saw First Uncle in winter, he would always have both hands buried inside his sleeves. I never saw him wearing either gloves or those cotton handwarmers that were a specialty of our hometown. From as early as I can remember—at least since I was ten—First Uncle's hands were always exposed to the cold, which meant that the backs of his hands were always cracked and bloody, each crack resembling the mouth of a crying baby. But First Uncle still needed to work, so he would do so with half-frozen hands. When he needed kindling, he would go to the hillside behind the village to collect it, or else he would collect dead branches from the tree in front of his house. He would then use this kindling to light a fire at home, so that his children could survive one bitterly cold winter after another.

First Uncle's children all became as calm and resilient in the face of adversity as First Uncle himself. The child who made the deepest impression on me was his second son, Shucheng. Although Shucheng was small, and every winter the backs of his hands would bleed, he wouldn't compete with others to get closer to the fire, and instead he would diligently go fetch more kindling. When there wasn't enough to eat, Shucheng wouldn't say a word but instead would just plop his empty bowl down onto the kitchen counter to express his dissatisfaction with that empty pot and with life in general. In general, he was very upright, persistent, and adamant. Although he spoke little, he was staunch and stoic and always appeared as solid as a stone.

Once, for some reason, First Uncle decided to beat Shucheng. First Uncle told him to kneel down in the center of the front room and then proceeded to slap him with a shoe, kick him, and beat him with a broomstick until it broke. All this was just to get Shucheng to say, "I was wrong, and I won't do it again." Through it all, Shucheng simply knelt there, not saying a word. Finally, he bit his lip, straightened his waist, and faced his father. First Uncle rarely cursed or beat his children, but that time he was infuriated. When he became so exasperated that he felt that if he didn't punish Shucheng for his insubordination he would be unable to preserve his self-respect as a father, then he had no choice but to beat his son.

For the entire time that it takes to eat half a bowl of rice, Shucheng—his face swollen, his mouth bloody, but his head held high—didn't say a word. Eventually, neighbors heard the ruckus and crowded around First Uncle's house, trying to keep First Uncle from erupting in anger again. First Uncle's own children knelt down, begging him to stop, and asking Shucheng, "Can't you just bow your head and admit you were wrong?"

Eventually, Shucheng responded.

He looked down at the children who were kneeling at his feet, then up at the crowd of neighbors gathered behind him. Finally, his gaze came to rest on First Uncle's face and the shoe First Uncle was holding and with which he had struck Shucheng's face countless times. Gritting his teeth, Shucheng said something that was not only historically apt but also left everyone completely astounded.

He said, "Go ahead and beat me. I'd rather die than be disgraced!"

Thinking back today on that beating and the words Shucheng shouted, I'm still flabbergasted; it's as though I've recalled a classic line from a film (like a scene from the Albanian film *Victory over Death*, known in Chinese as "I'd rather die than be disgraced"). But upon careful reflection, I realized that Shucheng's stubbornness and resilience were the product of that era's hardships; they were what had forged his survival instincts as well as First Uncle's own hardness. The ultimate consequence of that explosion was that those five or six children, at the urging of the neighbors, all rushed to First Uncle and knelt down before him. Their actions, however, further infuriated my uncle, increasing his useless gestures of resistance. What started out as First Uncle trying to punish Shucheng for his stubbornness and insubordination somehow ended up with him using the sole of his shoe to slap the faces of the children kneeling down in front of him. He cursed:

"If I kill all of you, our family's lives will improve . . ."

"If I kill all of you, I'll finally be able to relax . . ."

First Uncle continued to shout out these two lines every time he struck one of his children. To this day, the memory of First Uncle's livid expression, his trembling hands, and his shrill shouts makes me realize the pressure he must have felt from society and from life, which seemed to weigh down on him like a mountain—to the point that if he hadn't exploded like that, he could have been completely crushed by life's great pressure or smothered by his poverty.

He had exploded. He had erupted.

"If I kill all of you, our family's lives will improve . . ."

"If I kill all of you, I'll finally be able to relax . . ."

As First Uncle was shouting this, I stood terrified with the group of neighbors. I watched as he yelled and cursed, and after he had finished beating each of his children and was preparing to go another round, I—for some reason—emerged from the crowd and proceeded to kneel down next to his children. I hoped that, as he was beating his own children, he would beat me as well. By then I was already over ten years old, and as I knelt down with my cousins, tears began streaming down my face. I sobbed even more miserably than they did—and through my tears I watched First Uncle's shouts and beatings, which seemed to rain down from the sky like hail. Sobbing, I looked up and pleaded, "Uncle, please stop beating them."

First Uncle looked at me, his hand frozen in midair.

After a moment, he dejectedly sat down on a stool, and as he was putting his shoe back on he said, "Everyone get up and go eat. After you've finished eating, you can go out into the fields to turn some soil."

The explosion was finally contained. I got up and went to help First Uncle's children to their feet.

5. BUILDING A HOUSE

As I have noted, my father had two brothers and a cousin. First Uncle was the eldest, and his given name was Dayue ["large mountain"). My father was the second eldest, and his name was Shuangyue ["double mountain"). My father's cousin was the third eldest, and his name was Sanshuang ["third double"). My father's youngest brother was the fourth eldest uncle, and his name was Siyue ["fourth mountain"). The four of them lived so close together that First Uncle's family was at most a few dozen paces from our own. First Uncle's family would constantly come over to our house, and we would frequently go over to theirs.

Fourth Uncle worked away from home, and consequently First Uncle and my father would discuss Fourth Uncle's housework and other matters, after which First Uncle would go and attend to them.

When Father and First Uncle were discussing these matters, they could not avoid us children. When First Uncle came to our house, as soon as he stepped over the threshold, if it happened to be mealtime, Father would turn to Mother and say, "Go fetch Elder Brother a bowl."

Whenever Father and First Uncle discussed family matters, they didn't do so inside the house, but rather would sit outside under the eaves. It is indeed true that close relatives don't need to speak, and sincere words are seldom spoken, and precisely because Father and First Uncle were related and devoted to one another, they rarely spoke. It was as though with a single glance they could immediately know what the other was thinking.

On one such day, the early winter sun shone down on our family's courtyard, bathing everything in a golden glow. Father had spent half his life building the seven-room tile-roofed house for his four children, and in the 170-square-meter courtyard he had installed stone tiles with ripple patterns. It was in that stone-paved courtyard that First Uncle and Father ate together, and after they finished their food neither said a word. In fact, it wasn't until after I took the empty bowl from First Uncle that Father looked up at me and said, "Go serve yourself another bowl of rice." But when I went to refill my bowl, Elder Brother shook his head. I stood up and saw that Father looked as though there was something he had long wanted to say but hadn't been able to. Even after they had finished eating, and as First Uncle was about to leave, Father was still unable to get the necessary words out. First Uncle whispered to my father: "Shuangyue, Facheng (this was my uncle's eldest son) is already nineteen years old. Please tell Second Sister (which is to say, my mother) that if she finds someone appropriate, she should set him up with a wife."

My father gazed at First Uncle. After a silence, he nodded and whispered back, "A tile-roofed house . . . So, this year, you don't plan to build one?"

First Uncle stood in the middle of the courtyard and gazed up at the sky. He pondered for a moment and then replied, "Yes, we'll build one. We'll finish it in half a year."

These are the sorts of life matters that the two brothers discussed: building a house and finding wives for their sons, helping their children get married and establish their own families. Everything was very simple, and they understood each other implicitly. They treated each other with mutual understanding and mutual support. It was as if one of them had only to utter a few words, and the other would immediately risk his life to carry out his wishes. If one of them nodded to the other, this amounted to swearing an oath that he would do as requested.

It was directly from that simple exchange that my mother began asking around to try to find a wife for Facheng, while First Uncle began going to great effort to build a house. It was as if at that instant the two brothers suddenly understood that if the next generation was going to grow up successfully, the two of them were going to have to take responsibility for helping their children get married and establish their own families.

That was also the winter when, in order to build a three-room tile-roofed house, First Uncle and his children worked in the bitter cold throughout the whole season, and for the sake of building a house they endured wind and snow, conducting an extraordinary battle that would seal their fate. There was a mountain range seven or eight *li* to the west of our village that was part of Henan's Funiu mountain system. Western Henan is very hilly, and although in general the terrain is quite similar to that of Shaanxi's yellow loess plateau, this particular mountain range was full of distinctive formations of multilayer red rocks. If the hills were detonated with explosives, these stones would fracture into bright red bricks, which were the best resource one could use when it came to laying the foundation for a house. Therefore, the state organizations in our village—such as the commune, supply and marketing cooperative, wholesale department, and pharmacies—would generously purchase the stones in bulk, to use them to lay foundations for houses. But in order to haul the stones from that mountain, it was necessary to ford the Yi River, which was several hundred meters wide. There was no bridge spanning the river, and furthermore it was the middle of winter, so the only way to get the stones from one side to the other was for people to carry them across.

In order to build a house that winter, even as every other family crowded around the stove, First Uncle's family set to work. They repeatedly crossed the frozen river to haul back stones. The smaller stones weighed more than a hundred *jin*, and the larger ones weighed over a thousand, and everyone hauled as many as they could. Even when it was relatively warm, it was several degrees below zero, and when it was cold, the temperature could fall to ten or more degrees below. Both sides of the river were frozen solid, while in the middle, the water still flowed freely and fast and was bone-piercingly cold. In order to bring a stone from one side of the river to the other, it was necessary to ford the river. First Uncle would remove his clothes, so that he was wearing only underwear and a shirt. First he would stand on the riverbank and pound his frigid thigh muscles; then he would step into the water and proceed across the river, carrying a stone to the other bank. After it began to warm up and temperatures reached one or two degrees above zero, First Uncle and his children—with frost coming from their cold mouths and sweat on their brows, even as their bodies were covered in frozen water droplets—would carry stones through the waist-deep water to the other bank, and then they would return to the village.

That winter, First Uncle's family crossed that river again and again.

The following two winters, his family crossed the river in the same way, all in order to escape their frozen lives.

In the mountain ravines and wide rivers, the north wind blew, the grass withered, and tree branches swayed back and forth. Every household brought its cisterns inside, because otherwise the water inside would freeze and crack them. There was a continuous string of villages in the area—given that Henan led the nation in population density and my hometown region led the province in population density—but during those cold winters our entire village would effectively disappear, and no one would emerge from the houses unless it was absolutely necessary. However, not only did First Uncle and his children leave the village, they even went as far as the riverbank; and not only did they go to the riverbank, they even proceeded into the river, in temperatures that approached twenty degrees below zero. During those winters, whenever people saw First Uncle and his children, they would stare at them in astonishment and mumble, "Crazy! They've gone completely crazy!"

Or else they would exclaim, "My God, even if you don't care about yourself, you should at least care about your children!"

First Uncle wouldn't utter a word in response.

He wouldn't speak to passersby on the street and would rarely attempt to explain to other villagers the arduous labor in which he and his children were engaged. After the family hauled the stones back to the village, they would sell a portion to the village's work units and other institutions, and then would use the revenue to purchase bricks and tiles. They would take another portion of the stones back to the entranceway of their home to be used for the foundation of the new house.

During those winters, all the members of First Uncle's family used their bare hands to lift and haul stones; and, apart from when they returned home and crawled under the covers, they were usually walking barefoot over the stones on the riverside and stepping into the frozen river. As a result, their frozen hands and feet became thick and swollen, resembling fermented dough, with countless bloody cracks and reticulations. Near the end of each winter, there would be a pile of red square bricks under the two paulownia trees in front of First Uncle's house, and the pile would grow as tall as a person. It was as though First Uncle's family were stockpiling for a war on life. The stones gave off a fresh, frozen odor, such that everyone who walked by had to stop and look—and would remark on how excellent the stones were and how, if they were used for the foundation or the walls of a new house, they would be as neat and even as bricks but many times stronger. Then, the passersby would realize how industrious First Uncle's family had been. Because of their industriousness, they would be able to build the sort of house that everyone would admire. Having faith in time and fate, everyone would silently follow the construction of the house, until it stood tall at the end of the village and in the center of everyone's hearts.

6. APPRAISING A DAUGHTER-IN-LAW

Facheng, who is five or six years older than I am, is now already a grandfather. However, his children, and their entire generation, born in the eighties, will be unable to understand their father's generation—how its members struggled to survive, and how they set aside their dignity and comfort for the sake of marriage.

The process of appraising a potential spouse began after the Lunar New Year.

When First Uncle's new house was not yet built, Mother relied on a relative of a relative to make contact with a girl named Lianwa, from a village called Xiejiagou, which was located more than a dozen *li* away. Lianwa is now my cousin, and leads a very beautiful and fulfilled life. At the time, however, the first order was to convince her to marry into our family. I don't know how many times Mother, Father, and First Uncle discussed and planned this matter. For the day Lianwa would meet our family, Mother thoroughly swept the house inside and out, such that the only areas that remained unswept were the air inside the house and the trees in the courtyard. Mother also arranged for the people whom Lianwa would meet—such as First Uncle, First Aunt, and Facheng—to put on new clothes. She told me and my siblings and cousins—and particularly my younger cousins, who didn't have any clean clothes and, furthermore, didn't understand anything about clothing—to hide out in someone else's house.

Mother went to our house, took our brand-new red comforter from our bed, and then neatly folded it and placed it at the foot of First Uncle's bed. Second Sister filled our family's water kettles (which is to say, our thermoses) with hot water and took them to First Uncle's house, placing them on a table in the house's center room. She also washed several clean and unbroken bowls and placed them next to the water bottles, so that when the new bride-to-be arrived, she could use them as cups.

First Uncle's family also borrowed a new small table, which was painted red and to be used at mealtimes, and placed it in the center of the house. On the table they placed a bowl of peanuts and walnuts.

Of course, the protagonist of this exercise was my cousin Facheng. He put on a blue uniform, got a buzz cut, and waited at home for his prospective bride to arrive. Around noon, she entered the village, accompanied by a middle-aged woman. The prospective bride was shy and bashful, tall and thin—very presentable, and as simple and clear as lotus flowers. When she reached the front of the village, we all peeked at her from a distance, while some of the bolder children went up to her, pretending they were just passing by, and when they reached her they deliberately coughed, to startle her. And so, under everyone's watchful gaze, the two women entered the village and entered First Uncle's home. When the visitors reached that pile of stones that were going to be used to build a new house, I saw them look at the pile for a while, as if to confirm that they were in fact merely stones and not an actual three-room house.

I don't know what this lotus-blossom bride and Facheng said when they saw each other. I don't know what her thoughts and impressions of First Uncle's house were. In the end, after she ate lunch and left, the information that was transmitted back to us appeared to be that she had not consented to this marriage arrangement. It was not that she didn't accept Facheng himself, but rather that she didn't accept First Uncle's family.

She resented the family for being so poor.

She resented the family for being so large.

She resented the tile-roofed house for not yet being a tile-roofed house but merely a pile of stones.

After the women left, First Uncle came over to our house and sat in a room with my parents. I went into the room several times, and each time I saw that First Uncle's face was pale, as though a momentous event in his life had gone awry and had in turn impacted the fates of all the other members of his family. He sat there silently for a long time, but just as he was about to leave, he sighed and remarked, "Facheng's marriage arrangements were not successful, and I'm afraid our other children's arrangements will be even more difficult."

I don't know what First Uncle and Father discussed during that visit, but the next day Mother crossed the mountain to go see my future cousin, Lianwa. I don't know what my mother told Lianwa's family when she was there, but several days later, when our village was hosting a market day, Lianwa's father came to First Uncle's house to take a look. He walked through the house several times and even used his hand to measure the width of the paulownia trees in the courtyard. Finally, he came to a stop in front of that pile of stones and stood there for a long time. With one foot resting on the pile and the other one on the ground, he reflected for a while. Then he said to First Uncle, "That tree can be used as construction material."

First Uncle replied, "It will be used to build a house, and will provide wood for roof beams."

The other man then stared at the pile of stones, and said, "These stones were all hauled over from the river?"

First Uncle assented, then added, "When we can, we'll haul over several more carts, so that we can raise the foundation higher."

The other man suddenly said, "The marriage arrangements are hereby confirmed, but after I return home I'll have to convince my daughter."

First Uncle said, "This is the new society, and there is freedom of marriage. At the end of the day, children must make their own decision."

In retrospect, it's clear that Lianwa's marriage to Facheng amounted to her winning the rural marriage lottery. At that time, Facheng was only eighteen or nineteen years old, but he had already established a reputation as an excellent bricklayer, and now he has become a so-called manager and labor contractor for the rural construction brigade. He is a good man and very capable and is able to ensure his family can live a good life. Everything he touches turns to gold, and he is loved by everyone he meets. However, I remember how anxious First Uncle had been thirty years earlier about this marriage and how, after Lianwa's family finally agreed to the marriage, First Uncle had come over to our house with a bright smile and asked my mother, "They've agreed?"

Mother replied, "Yes, but they want to wait until the house is finished. They say that one should definitely get married and move straight into a new tile-roofed house."

When he heared that, First Uncle's smile immediately faded— it was like someone suddenly stumbling while walking. No longer smiling, and instead nodding, he solemnly replied, "Then please tell them that I said I would build a house, and I will definitely keep my word."

It has already been three years since First Uncle died. Even if he were still alive, he might no longer remember that solemn promise. This is because throughout the first half—or even the first two-thirds—of his life, he continually struggled to keep his promises while continuing to make new ones. First Uncle was someone who tried to keep his word and who endured endless frustration when he was unable to do so.

For more than half his life, First Uncle was tortured by the promises he made, but it was also for the sake of these promises that he lived, and they revealed the nobility and vulgarity of his humble peasant's view of life. These promises showed how First Uncle would leave a deeper and brighter mark than others on the land and on the road of life.

7. DIGNITY

That year, construction on the house began.

That year, Facheng's marriage arrangements were confirmed.

On the day the house was completed, we followed local custom and invited all the workers and craftsmen over to eat and drink. Everyone ate meat and drank liquor, and after they departed, the new three-room tile-roofed house on the side of the road was left empty and quiet. It was filled with a reddish-green mixture of the scents from the bricks and stones combined with the moist and fragrant smell of mud. The building was completely empty. The early summer sun poured in through the window, illuminating those beautiful odors as though shining onto an invisible sheet of silk. As my relatives and I were standing and sitting in that new house, admiring the sunlight and beginning to have a muddled sense of optimism toward life, First Uncle entered.

First Uncle said, "Since all of you are here now, I want to tell you a few things." More than 170 centimeters tall, he stood in the sunny entryway like a tree. He reminded me of Chairman Mao standing at the gate tower at Tiananmen Square. On October 1, 1949, Chairman Mao had overlooked the square and declared, "New China has been established! The Chinese people have risen to their feet!" More than two decades later, a northern peasant stood in the doorway of the house that he and his family had painstakingly built with their own sweat and blood and announced to his six sons and two daughters, "The house is now complete, but we have incurred some debts. In this world, you can owe anything, but the one thing you shouldn't owe is a monetary debt. Beginning tomorrow, we will once again begin hauling and selling stones, so as to quickly repay our debts."

Life got back on track, as though it had never been derailed. Every day, First Uncle's family would wake up in the morning before dawn and travel to the river more than ten *li* away, where they would go to the gully on the other side of the river to collect stones. After collecting the stones they would ford the waist-deep water to return to their side of the river, and would then sell the stones to the state work units. Each day they would make two round trips—setting out each morning when the night sky was still full of stars and returning home each night when the sky was once again full of stars. Apart from the Lunar New Year and periods when there was a lot of farm work, First Uncle and his family proceeded like this, day after day, year after year. In all, they continued like this for three years, their own version of China's Three Years of Natural Disasters.

Because of this process of constructing the new house, First Uncle's family experienced many highs and lows, revealing the ways in which his family resembled and differed from those of his neighbors. Their similarity lay in the fact that they all experienced the grinding and difficult rural life of that era, while their difference was that, because First Uncle had a large family, his family's days were even more harrowing and exhausting than those of his neighbors. Thanks to First Uncle, his family resembled a newly sprouted forest in which a strong old tree gives the entire forest shape and form, spirit and character. First Uncle was, of course, the strong old tree. He labored like an ox, and he led his children as though they were a flock of geese. Moreover, he always made a particular effort to make sure his children had more to eat and that their clothing was less tattered than would otherwise have been the case, and he made sure that when his children grew up they would all have the opportunity to get married and establish their own family. In this respect, First Uncle, despite the fact that he couldn't read and was disinclined to discuss matters in any real depth, truly understood the meaning and implications of one crucial concept: dignity.

That is to say, the dignity that people are able to achieve while living on this earth.

It is possible to speak of there being differing amounts of dignity but not of differences in the *essence* of dignity. It is like the way clocks tell time. Some clocks are as large as a house and as tall as a pine tree, while others are as small as a fist or an egg, and when placed on a table or at the head of a bed they resemble a sparrow sitting on a branch. Among wristwatches, at the time there was the Zhongshan brand from Nanjing, which was the size of a copper coin and appeared light yellow in the sunlight. These sold for thirty yuan each, and when you wore one on your wrist it looked distinctive, if somewhat crass. There was also the Shanghai brand, which sold for more than a hundred yuan each and appeared truly refined and exquisite. There were also imported watches, such as the ultrathin transparent ones from Japan or the beautiful, smooth ones from Switzerland. These various kinds of clocks and watches can be distinguished on the basis of their size, expense, and appearance, but in the end they are alike in that they all measure hours, minutes, and seconds, which is to say, the accumulation of dispersed life and existence. Meanwhile, dignity—of life and of people—is just like the time you see on a clock or watch, in that timepieces may differ, but the actual time they keep remains the same. In fact, this is even more the case with dignity. A king's dignity is not inherently greater than that of an ordinary person, just as the dignity of a provincial governor is not inherently more valuable than that of a rural peasant.

I thought, if it is true that a king, for the sake of his own dignity, can decapitate someone, while commoners, to assert their dignity, must struggle to keep their backs straight while being decapitated, in order to show that their lives are not trivial and debased—then the dignity of the latter is, in fact, more worthy of respect than that of the former.

If a provincial governor, for the sake of his dignity, can mercilessly send down a directive claiming for himself the labor and the wealth of countless people, while peasants, for the sake of their dignity, must simply sharpen their scythes even more quickly and make their plow blades even sharper—in that case, the dignity of the latter will similarly be even more valuable than that of the former.

This is the way the world is. In the name of dignity, an emperor can go to war, while commoners have no choice but to continue to labor.

The rich, in the name of dignity, can gamble away thousands of taels on a single throw of the dice, while the poor, in the name of dignity, must struggle to keep their begging bowl clean while fleeing from catastrophe.

For a tree, dignity is managing not to topple over during a storm, while for a blade of grass dignity is striving to become as green as possible in the springtime and deferring the withering process as long as possible in autumn. For a house, dignity involves being lived in, while for a car, dignity involves being able to go fast even when carrying a full load. For a dog, dignity involves being able to avoid having neighbors or passersby kick it or throw rocks at it, while for a cat, dignity means not having a rat scurry by in front of it unscathed. A grain of sand by the side of the road might appear to be lifeless, but it still has dignity, and its dignity lies in its ability to avoid being blown away by the wind like a speck of dust; and even if the grain of sand is blown away, the dust will always be blown first, and therefore the sand's dignity lies in its being stronger and more resilient than dust.

Dignity is the time of life, but it is also the portion and weight accorded to life within one's allotted time. Dignity is not invisible air and drifting clouds, but rather it is the spirit of life itself.

Dignity isn't simply displayed in life's clothing and appearance, but it is contained, more importantly, in life's inner strength and integrity.

First Uncle was an extremely dignified person.

He was a commoner who placed a number-one priority on people's dignity.

As a peasant, he was the member of our production brigade with the best farming skills and the best crops.

As a man, and for the sake of his honor, he once took a cleaver, went over to a neighboring village several *li* away, and chopped off someone's ear.

As a father, he was constantly working and sweating, every year, every month, and every instant—and was determined that his eight children, despite growing up in an extremely impoverished era, wouldn't miss out on the opportunity to grow up and get married.

First Uncle led his children, and together they used their sweat and blood to repay his debt within a year of having completed that three-room tile-roofed house. After paying off his debt, First Uncle proceeded to collect, under the gable of the new house, a pile of bricks and stones to be used to build yet another house. Just as he was building up that new pile of stones, First Uncle's eldest son, Cousin Facheng, and Lianwa got married. There were drums and fireworks, peanuts and walnuts, couplets and colorful confetti, together with endless streams of rural residents and piles of laughter that rose above the impoverished land—they all welcomed the new bride of the eldest of First Uncle's six sons. Just as everyone was carrying the bride and groom into their new house, and all were crowding around talking and laughing, First Uncle summoned my mother over to a quiet corner of the house and solemnly said, "My second son, Shucheng, is also grown up, so if you know of anyone appropriate, please introduce him. Please tell the other family that after Shucheng gets married, I'll definitely build him his own house."

8. GAMBLING

We find that First Uncle was quite confident of his own tenacity and was willing to say so in front of anyone. When it came to dignity, however, First Uncle never dared to claim he was the most dignified person in the village.

This is because . . . he liked to gamble.

Gambling was First Uncle's weakness. It was a weakness that contaminated his moral character—like a wound in his spirit that would never heal.

In our hometown, low-stakes gambling was viewed as a form of rural entertainment or even as a cultural activity undertaken during the periods of the New Year holiday and the harvest rest. However, for First Uncle, low-stakes gambling became high-stakes gambling, and once he began gambling round-the-clock, not returning home to eat or sleep, to the point that when he lost he'd ask everyone for money and would even sell his grain and his trees—by then, gambling was no longer merely a form of entertainment but rather a kind of addiction.

It was from recreational betting that First Uncle first entered a life of gambling. Initially, because he was exhausted during the farming season and idle during the slack season, he joined some other villagers to play a wagering game known as "flipping three hats." This involved taking three coins and polishing the reverse side of each one until it was shiny, while the front side would still have the characters for the emperor Qianlong or Daoguang. Then, a player would take these three coins and hold them such that the side with writing was facing up and the polished side facing down. Half bowing, he would throw the coins onto a stone or brick on the ground. If all three coins landed with the polished side up, this would count as a win; if one coin landed with the writing facing up, this would count as a partial loss. This was a simple game with rules that could be easily explained and quickly learned.

Initially, First Uncle would wager only a few cents per game, but later he moved up to several dozen cents, or even several yuan per game. He would gamble until his eyes were bloodshot, and eventually his wagers would increase to one or two hundred yuan. Of course, today some people might spend a hundred yuan on a pack of cigarettes, and two or three hundred yuan on a meal in a street-side restaurant. But in the sixties and seventies—when small eggs cost only two or three cents, large ones cost only three or four cents, and an entire *jin* of salt cost only eight cents—to lose one or two hundred yuan was like losing the equivalent of a one-room house, while losing two or three hundred yuan was like losing the equivalent of a three-room tile-roofed house or a complex with a courtyard.

Nevertheless, every year First Uncle would gamble and lose, and then he would gamble some more. The size of his bets was such that every year he would lose the equivalent of a three-room house or a complex with a courtyard. In fact, every year during the New Year holiday, he would take all the savings he had painstakingly earned by going out with his children and braving wind and snow to cross the icy river and collect stones from the opposite bank—money that had been earmarked for building houses for his sons, so that they might be able to find a wife and get married—and after finishing his New Year's dumplings he would disappear without a trace. Eventually, his wife or children would have to go to the gambling den to drag him home.

In order to prevent First Uncle from gambling on New Year's Eve, First Aunt would carefully hide all the family's savings—but regardless of where she hid the money, First Uncle would always find it.

First Uncle, in order to prevent himself from gambling, would give my parents whatever extra money he had. He would ask them to put it away, telling them that if one day he were to suffer a large gambling loss and ask them for it back, under no circumstances should they give it to him, and instead should keep it for when his children were ready to get married. But in the end the result was always the same: First Uncle's plan would backfire, and the next time he lost everything at the gambling table, he would invariably come to my parents and say, "Please give me back the money. I need it for an emergency."

My parents would know he had been gambling, but they still couldn't refuse his request.

Mother would say, "Brother, you must stop gambling."

First Uncle's face would turn bright red. He would say, "It's not for gambling. I really do have an emergency."

Father was First Uncle's younger brother, and First Uncle's gambling would infuriate Father to the point that he would stomp his feet and even lose his appetite. I thought, if only Father were First Uncle's elder brother, then when First Uncle came to ask for money to support his gambling habit, Father would be able to slap him in the face. Similarly, if Father had been a generation older than First Uncle, then he could have responded to his gambling habit by kicking him out of the house or hanging him from the rafters. But Father was the younger brother, and consequently the dictates of rural ethics and morality left him angry, frustrated, and helpless. Whenever First Uncle suffered gambling losses and asked Father for his money back, or else went to Mother to ask if he could borrow twenty or thirty yuan, Father would always turn away, bow his head, and shed a few tears. After Father's tears dried or were wiped away, he would turn back to First Uncle and say, "Brother, can't you just stop gambling?"

First Uncle would stand silently in front of him for a while, and then would say, with great shame, "After this, I promise I'll stop."

Because First Uncle was Father's elder brother, Father had no choice but to give him back the money. As First Uncle left the house with the money to go gamble, Father would watch his departing shadow, and even if he didn't shed a tear, his face would always turn bright red, as though he had been crying.

9. SEEKING THE SHORT ROAD OUT

There was one particular occasion when First Uncle lost a lot of money. He left home on the second day of the Lunar New Year, and when he returned on the third, his face was pale and his eyes dull. He returned home and sat in the middle of his room without saying a word. Needless to say, he had not only lost money while gambling—possibly all the money he had set aside to build houses in preparation for his sons' weddings—he had also lost his dignity and his reputation. The loss of money is not unimportant, but sometimes the loss of one's dignity and reputation can be far more consequential. This is because one's reputation and dignity don't merely concern one's own character and standing, they also influence the ability of one's children to establish their own families. To help his children get married, First Uncle had been more conscientious and had worked much harder than most other fathers—precisely because he understood that his reputation as a gambler could influence his children's ability to find spouses and establish their own families. In fact, his reputation as a gambler did indeed damage his family's reputation and his children's ability to find spouses. When the young women who initially expressed interest in marrying his sons learned about First Uncle's gambling habit, they either were unwilling to proceed with the marriage or at the least became very hesitant. So when First Uncle returned home on the afternoon of that third day of the new year, he didn't say a word or do a thing. He didn't discuss eating or being hungry, nor did he discuss sleeping or being tired. Instead, he simply sat there without moving, until finally his family approached and asked:

"Did you lose again?"

"How much did you lose?"

No matter how many times they asked, First Uncle still wouldn't utter a word in response. Finally, when it reached the point that he seemed to have no alternative but to answer, but he still remained unable to say anything, First Uncle suddenly began slapping his own face. He hit and cursed himself, exclaiming that he'd lost all trace of dignity and that he might as well die.

First Uncle was a firm and upstanding person, and he had never before experienced this sense of utter despair and self-loathing. Therefore, when his family saw him like this, they were all terrified. They rushed forward to grab his hands, saying that no matter how much money he might have lost, he should simply resolve to stop gambling. His children, their eyes full of tears, urged him not to beat himself, saying that it wasn't a big deal if the family had to spend another year going down to the river to haul stones in order to earn back the money.

That was how things stood. Earlier, First Uncle had already succeeded in raising virtually all the money he needed to build a second house, and it had been agreed that construction would begin after the New Year holiday. But now the family stopped mentioning the new house at all, and instead they had to continue going down to that riverbank ten *li* away to haul back stones like beasts of burden.

The family continued in this way, waiting for the day when they would once again have enough money to build a new house. One day that summer, when the sun was blazing so hot that steam was rising from the ground, and the cries of the cicadas were gushing forth like running water, I returned from school carrying my book bag. As soon as I stepped into the courtyard, I shouted, "Mother, I'm dying of thirst!"

All I heard was silence.

I had a sense that something momentous had happened. I rushed inside and I saw my parents and my sisters sitting there silently.

I asked, "What happened?"

Mother took my book bag and replied with a single word, "Gambling."

I went to see First Uncle. Our houses were only a dozen paces apart, with just a couple of houses in between, and so it took only a few moments to reach his house. There were many neighbors on the road, but I proceeded as though I were going through empty fields or along a mountain path. My heart felt empty and desolate, as though a load of sand had suddenly fallen onto my chest, such that I could hear my own heart beating. This was the first time in my life that I would see someone who had just attempted suicide. I was afraid for my first uncle—who, for as long as I could remember, had loved this poor, rural life and had loved all his children and nieces and nephews. I couldn't understand why anyone had to gamble or why, once you were hooked, it was virtually impossible to extricate yourself. If you couldn't break the habit, it could either drive your

family to ruin or drive you to suicide, and First Uncle chose the latter. Just as I was about to reach his house, I silently warned myself,
Lianke, you must make sure never to gamble!

I arrived at First Uncle's house.

First Uncle's house was just like ours—everyone was sitting
silently in the main room. After entering I looked around, then asked
quietly, "Where's my uncle?" Someone glanced at the inner room. I
followed that person's gaze and entered the other room. The inner
room was much darker than the outer one, and the rays of light were
very dim, like the breath of a sick person. I stood in the doorway for
a moment, staring blankly, until finally I managed to see First Uncle,
lying on the bed against the back wall. He was facing the inner wall,
with his back to the door.

I quietly said, "First Uncle," and walked over to his bed.

First Uncle made a slight movement but didn't turn over.

I stood there next to his bed. I very much wanted to act as an
adult and ask him whether he was feeling better. I very much wanted
to tell him that if he wanted to gamble he could do so, but that there
was no need for him to try to take his own life. In the end, I didn't
say a word, and instead I just stood there. I don't know how long I
stood there, but eventually, as though bored, I turned around and
started to walk out. At that moment, First Uncle was roused, perhaps
by the sound of me turning away. He suddenly rolled over, grasped
my hand, and then caressed my face. In a soft yet clear voice, he
said, "You can continue your studies without worries. Uncle won't
gamble anymore."

When I heard First Uncle say this, tears immediately began
to stream down my face. First Uncle had only lost his property, but
even if—in addition to gambling—he had also been killing and steal-
ing, he would nevertheless still be my uncle and one of my closest
relatives. When I emerged from his house, my face was soaked with

tears and my heart was as warm as the mountains are high and the rivers are long, and it was overflowing like the sea. Even today, when I remember First Uncle's suicide attempt, the fraternal ties between Father, First Uncle, and Fourth Uncle, and the gains and losses they each endured for the sake of the most ordinary existence—I can appreciate how, as someone grows older, the most important consideration is not issues of material comfort or spiritual vicissitudes but rather that drizzle-like warmth and moisture that is produced by a combination of material and spiritual sustenance. This is similar to how plants won't grow if they lack water and sunlight, but on the other hand if they are confronted with torrential rains combined with scorching heat, they still won't flourish and instead will only generate unproductive overgrowth. Instead, it is only under the moisture and nourishment of that type of light drizzle, and under the light and warmth of that sort of daylight, that grass can become grass, trees can become trees, and people's souls can become hearts full of warmth and goodness.

I grew up in a household full of poverty and warmth.

My cousins also grew up in households full of poverty and warmth. Altogether I had fifteen first cousins on my father's side and more than twenty second cousins. Including myself, however, there wasn't anyone in the family who succeeded in becoming an official, or who became so rich that for them money flowed like water. At the same time, there also wasn't anyone who wasn't a fundamentally good person, nor was there anyone who didn't attempt—after establishing a solid moral foundation—to overlay other colors onto this foundation, so that their lives would be further enriched by friendship and full of happiness and warmth.

Goodness was the foundation and the basis of our humanity.

After I returned home from First Uncle's house, my mother gave me a summary of First Uncle's decision to try to take his own life. She described how he had gone to calculate how much his family had earned over the preceding year from selling stones to various different work units, whereupon he happened to run into some former gambling buddies. One thing led to another, and before he knew it several of them had decided to go to an old favorite spot, and there First Uncle lost all of his money. No one knows what precisely First Uncle thought and did after losing all of his money, or what kind of struggle and torment he must have gone through. In any case, First Uncle returned home just as the villagers were about to take an after-lunch nap. As usual, whenever he ran into someone he knew, he would chat with them. As usual, he stopped by the front door of his house, looked around, and then told a child to go find all the children from First Uncle's family and from his relatives' families who weren't in school, and tell them to assemble in the shade beneath the toon tree by the side of the road. He then took handful after handful of candy out of his pocket and distributed it to the children. After each child had received a handful, he asked who hadn't gotten any, and the children held up their candy and replied they had all received some. Then First Uncle asked who wasn't present, whereupon he noticed that my eldest sister's daughter Yuanyuan was missing, so he sent another child to go find her.

When Yuanyuan arrived, she greeted him, saying "Granddad," whereupon he took out a handful of candies from his pocket and handed them to her. Then he smiled and asked the children whether they had eaten candied fruit before, and they all smiled and indicated that they had. First Uncle looked again at the children and patted their heads and faces. After the children had finished their candy, they departed like a flock of geese. With one of his pockets emptied of the candies he had bought for the children and the other full of rat poison he had purchased for himself, First Uncle returned home, closed the door, and proceeded to swallow the poison. Shortly after,

First Aunt happened to return from washing clothes and found her husband lying on the bed, his mouth full of white foam, so she immediately called out for someone to help take him to the hospital.

First Uncle was successfully resuscitated. But up to this day, every time I remember that—before trying to seek the short road out by taking his own life—First Uncle had given each of his grandchildren, grandnieces, and grandnephews a handful of candy, my heart becomes filled with sweetness and warmth. I was truly blessed to have had Father and my uncles in my life. While I was growing up, virtually the only thing I didn't lack was a feeling of warmth and protection.

10. TELEVISION

After that incident, First Uncle didn't gamble for a long time. Even during the Lunar New Year, when he became so bored that he didn't know what to do with himself, he would just go down to the gambling hall and stroll around.

Before I finished high school, I dropped out of school and went to work in the train station and the cement factory in Xinxiang. Then, in 1978, I joined army units stationed in Henan's Shangqiu, Kaifeng, and other places. Several years later, when I returned from the army to visit my family, I went to give my uncle some health tonics, whereupon I sat down with him in another new tile-roofed house he had just built. First Uncle told me that he sold scallions, garlic, and melons. He noted that business was better than before, and he was able to earn more money. He said that sometimes when the apples were in season, he would go to Lingbao county in Henan's Sanmenxia City and bring back apples to sell at home, or else he would take a car to as far away as Hubei or Sichuan to purchase tangerines and bring them back in order to sell them to local shops and fruit stands.

First Uncle said he was able to earn quite a bit of money in this way.

I gazed at him with a concerned expression.

First Uncle laughed, and added, "Don't worry, I won't gamble. I definitely won't gamble."

My concern was slowly allayed—as the concern of a child dangling in midair who is then carefully lowered to the ground. First Uncle gestured toward the newly built house and said that even after having constructed it, he still had several hundred yuan saved up, and he hoped that when I returned the following year I might be able to pull some strings and help him purchase a television through some backdoor connections. He said that if he had a television to keep him company during the boring slack season, then not only would he not gamble, he wouldn't even have any interest in going to the gambling hall to stroll around. However, he said that without a television, during the slack season he wouldn't be able to resist going to the gambling hall to look around, and if he did so, he was concerned he might be unable to resist taking up gambling again.

I nodded and agreed that the next time I returned home to visit my family, I would definitely get First Uncle a television. That was the mid-eighties, and televisions were among China's most popular products. So in order to buy First Uncle a television, upon returning to the army I immediately set about developing my social *guanxi*.

11. TIECHENG

The real assault on First Uncle began in the early eighties.

In the early eighties, First Uncle's fifth child, Tiecheng, followed in my footsteps and joined the army. The difference was that I was posted in Henan, which meant I was essentially stationed in my own hometown. Tiecheng, however, ended up being assigned to a battalion stationed in Urumqi, in distant Xinjiang. By train, it took six days and seven nights—or seven days and six nights—to reach that desolate borderland.

From when he was young, Tiecheng had always been quiet and introverted, and he was someone who would repeatedly get worked up over inconsequential things. Precisely because he was too fastidious, he would often get upset over minor things, just like a girl. This is why First Uncle and my father decided to encourage him to join the army, so that he could receive training and pursue his ambitions. Accordingly, shortly before the end of the year, he put on his uniform and, with several other youths from the village, went to join the battalion in Urumqi. But after only ten days or two weeks of training, Tiecheng hanged himself.

He was just eighteen years old.

He died at the end of the year, but it wasn't until the end of the first month of the following year that the news finally made it back to us. The strange circumstances surrounding his death gave us a terrible feeling of pain and bitterness. In the first month of the new year, someone in our village had woken up early and gone out for a walk, when they found a letter lying in the middle of the road in front of Tiecheng's house. Noting that First Uncle was listed as the addressee, though there was no return address, the person delivered the letter to First Uncle's house. When First Uncle opened it, it was as if an explosion had blasted through his home, while his entire family stared in shock.

Apart from reporting that Tiecheng had committed suicide, the letter didn't contain any other information. It didn't include a signature or a date, nor did it specify the reason for the suicide, or even the time he had been found. Just as First Uncle's family, weeping and sobbing, was attempting to use telegrams and telephone calls to confirm the letter's authenticity, and as my cousin Facheng was preparing to go to Luoyang to buy a train ticket to Urumqi, someone from the county's department of military affairs accompanied by an army cadre brought an urn with Tiecheng's ashes to First Uncle's house. They explained that a couple of weeks after Tiecheng had joined the battalion and begun training, because the battalion had not been marching well, the commander in charge of new recruits had stomped on Tiecheng's foot. Tiecheng had found himself at a loss, so he had returned to his dormitory and hanged himself with a cord from his backpack.

They claimed that the commander had only lightly tapped his foot a few times.

They didn't specify whether or not this report that the commander had only lightly stepped on his foot was accurate.

Nor did they specify what responsibility Tiecheng's military commander should accept for the loss of this life.

They had even less to say about why, if Tiecheng died at the end of the year, it wasn't until the latter half of the following month that the news finally reached our family—and why they didn't permit our family to go to the scene and witness Tiecheng's cremation, and instead they merely sent us his ashes.

One moment, his life was fresh, like a drop of dew illuminated by the morning sun, but a month later that person was no more, and there wasn't even a corpse. Instead, there was only an ice-cold urn full of ashes. Responding to our heartrending cries, a military cadre contacted us, saying that the primary responsibility for Tiecheng's suicide lay in the fact that he was not sufficiently open-minded. The cadre promised that although ordinarily a suicide would be classified as a natural death, as long as First Uncle's family agreed not to pursue the matter further, Tiecheng's case could be classified as a death in the line of duty, meaning that he could be designated a martyr.

With this, the matter was considered concluded.

It was only a few months after Tiecheng's death that I learned about all these developments.

When I returned home to visit my family, as soon as my parents saw me, they immediately proceeded to give me a detailed account of this incident, with all its twists and turns. By that point I had already been promoted to the position of army cadre and was working in the political department of the division office, and I was therefore intimately familiar with every detail relating to our so-called Pure Land military barracks. So I put down my luggage, had a drink of water, and went to First Uncle's house.

In First Uncle's house, there was a table with Tiecheng's ashes and funeral portrait. His children had all gone to work in the fields. The early summer air was fresh and clear, and when it drifted over from the fields it soaked me and First Uncle like a flood. Under the courtyard windows, there was a Chinese toon tree with a trunk as wide as a bowl, which cast a shadow that stretched into the room through the doorway. There was the strange odor of toon leaves and sap, and as I entered the house, the hospital smell of bicarbonate of soda seeped out from under the door. Surrounded by these strange odors, First Uncle and I sat silently for what seemed like ages. It was as though Tiecheng's funeral portrait standing on the table was staring at me, waiting for me to break this silence and say something on his behalf.

Finally, I remarked that it appeared perhaps his death wasn't so simple. I suggested that we shouldn't be so quick to agree to his superiors' request and let this incident pass like the sun rising in the morning and setting in the evening. I added that even if it was true that Tiecheng committed suicide, he must have had his reasons, and we should demand that the army address our queries.

I brought up many other things, including that the letter notifying us of Tiecheng's death lacked a return address, and speculated that it must be that the army wanted to suppress the news, and that they were afraid we would take advantage of the New Year holiday to travel to Xinjiang to investigate—which was why they didn't permit the other new recruits, including one from Tiecheng's own hometown, to write to us and tell us about this incident. The other recruit from the same hometown must have felt an acute sense of frustration and an obligation to help someone from the same hometown, so he belatedly sent that letter, and after his parents read it, they secretly left it in the entranceway to Tiecheng's house, in order to convey the news to his family.

I offered First Uncle many different thoughts and perspectives, and was even going to tell him how, in the army, older soldiers often used corporal punishment to break in new recruits, and how these sorts of complications were difficult to prevent. Just as I was about to say this, I looked up at First Uncle sitting there in front of me, and I noticed that a layer of sweat had appeared on his haggard and sallow forehead—making it look as though he were running a high fever.

I said, "First Uncle, are you ill?"

First Uncle shook his head.

I said, "So, are you just going to leave the issue of Tiecheng's death like this?"

Gazing at me, First Uncle remained silent for a long time, until finally he replied in a soft voice: "If we go to the army to file a complaint, I know someone will be punished and a powerful military officer will be fired. But would this bring Tiecheng back to life? I inquired, and know that those military officers and brigade leaders all came from the countryside. They all found themselves in desperate circumstances at home, which is why they had no choice but to join the army and be sent to the remote Xinjiang borderland. They were all attempting to improve their lives. Your cousin is already dead, and there's no need for us to destroy other people's future prospects."

At this point, First Uncle turned toward Tiecheng's memorial altar and gazed at his son's photograph. Finally, after appearing to reach an agreement with the photograph, he turned back and looked at me for a while. Then he sighed and added, "Because our family hasn't spoken up and asked anything, the army might think that we are pushovers. Other villagers may assume we didn't file a report because we were hoping Tiecheng would be designated a martyr. But if that is the case, then so be it. Let them think whatever they wish. In any event, this is what I have decided. Our family has endured a tragedy, but there is no need for us to bring others down in the process."

As I emerged from First Uncle's house, I truly appreciated his goodness and magnanimity. I knew that his heartbreak was like a bottomless well, but his speech and actions reflected a broad-minded outlook that was as vast as the endless fields. At that moment I respected and even venerated him. First Uncle was an ordinary person, and although people often said that he had a gambling problem, while I watched him handle Tiecheng's affairs after his death, I truly felt that he was the most extraordinary person in our village, and even in the entire world.

12. LIANYUN

In any event, Tiecheng's death appeared to have shattered a link in First Uncle's chain of fate. After the suicide, First Uncle appeared to age precipitously, and he lost a considerable amount of weight. He seldom spoke with other villagers, and his hair immediately turned gray. When he saw the other children from his clan, he would still give them candy and toys he had bought from street stalls, but when he did so his eyes would fill with tears as he gazed in the direction of the hillside where we had buried Tiecheng's ashes.

People who have experienced a tragedy cannot simply excise the memory from their life. Instead, they have no choice but to try to carry on as before. They will still have three meals a day, four seasons a year. Each day may have a different number of daylight hours, and each season may be colder or warmer than the others—but in the end an individual or a family cannot expect more charity just because they have experienced a tragedy. Even if an entire nation, or a people, undergoes a devastating tragedy, the earth will continue orbiting the sun. In spring, First Uncle still needed to sow the fields; in summer, he still needed to weed and irrigate the crops; and during the slack season, he still needed to sell onions, garlic, and apples. First Uncle's dream was to bring his children to this earth and then exert every effort to help each of them get married and establish his or her own family.

First Uncle was still determined to build each of his sons a new three-room tile-roofed house. He was also determined to prepare a full dowry for each of his two daughters, so that both could leave their family home and join their in-laws, like other young women. Although in the end First Uncle was unable to complete all these goals, he did his best. When he was sixty, he was still running to buy apples, bananas, and oranges from elsewhere and bringing them back to his hometown to sell them. He earned and lost money doing so every year. On some trips he might have good luck and make a profit, but each year there would inevitably be one or two trips on which he would lose money. For instance, once he brought back a load of oranges from Hubei, but another merchant had brought a load back from Sichuan a few days earlier and was able to sell his for a much lower price. Therefore, First Uncle had no choice but to repeatedly discount his oranges until in the end he was virtually giving them away. As a result, he lost in one fell swoop all the profits he had earned from his previous few trips. On another occasion, he went to eastern Henan to purchase some seedless watermelons and bring them back to our home in western Henan, but after he returned there was a long stretch of rainy weather, and he had to watch those watermelons rot in his house. In the end, he dumped them into a ditch in front of his house as though dumping a cartful of mud.

First Uncle's daily struggles for survival left him going in circles like an idling motor, unable to advance.

Whenever First Uncle succeeded in earning some money, the heavens would make certain he would suffer serious losses; and because he had suffered losses, he would then have to scramble and collect some capital so that he might have a chance to make another profit. In the end, he continued rushing around like this, with each loss followed by a gain, and each gain eventually followed by another loss. His situation resembled that of Sisyphus, and it was no longer important whether or not Sisyphus would be able to push that stone up to the mountaintop; the important thing was his fate and experience. Experience is the entirety of life, and although in and of itself it may not have much significance, in the end it is life itself. First Uncle's life exemplified this; whenever he made a profit it would be followed by a loss, and whenever he suffered a loss he would have to follow it up with a solid profit. Every time was a new beginning, and he would set off again from where he had previously stopped. He continued in this way until a new disaster finally brought that endless cycle to a halt.

Once, when First Uncle's youngest child—his second daughter, who was always laughing and optimistic—went with him to the neighboring county of Lingbao to sell apples, she was killed in a car accident. This disaster befell First Uncle and his family a little over a year after Tiecheng's suicide. On the day in question, it was already dusk, and the car in which First Uncle and his daughter were hauling apples had stopped by the side of the road, whereupon a large truck rushed toward them from the opposite direction. The driver had been drinking, and the truck smashed into First Uncle's car as it drove by. My cousin, who was standing by the side of the road, cried out—it turned out to be her last utterance on this earth.

In this way, my cousin, who was only seventeen years old at the time, departed from this world and went to join her brother Tiecheng.

With this, First Uncle stopped engaging in that sort of circular trading.

With this, First Uncle would frequently lapse into silence. He would sit alone in front of the village, gazing out at the hill where my two cousins were buried. No one knew what he was thinking, nor did they grasp his understanding of life, fate, and mortality.

I learned of my cousin's death one day in mid-autumn. I was in the family courtyard of the military office in Kaifeng, when someone suddenly told me I had a visitor waiting at my front door. I hurried home and saw that First Uncle was sitting exhaustedly on a cement step under a holly tree in front of my building. I rushed up to him, but at the last moment I stopped and called out in surprise, "First Uncle!"

First Uncle didn't reply and instead merely turned and gave me a bitter smile.

I asked, "Why have you come?"

First Uncle still didn't say a word, and instead just gazed at me helplessly.

I quickly opened the door and led him inside. I told him to sit down on a couch. According to our hometown custom, I didn't immediately offer him some water nor did I offer to brew him some tea, as I would an ordinary visitor. Our family didn't come from a tea-producing region, so some of us didn't have the habit of drinking tea. Instead, I turned on the gas stove and proceeded to boil him some eggs. When I brought over the eggs, First Uncle gazed at me and said, in a very calm voice, "Lianke, your cousin Lianyun is dead. She had a car accident in Lingbao county."

I stared in shock.

There was a thud in my head. I stood in the center of my ten-square-meter living room staring at First Uncle. I don't know why, but I abruptly had an urge to kneel down in front of him. I wanted to curl up in his lap and weep. But instead I remained as motionless as a wooden plank. For a long time, I didn't say a word, as tears ran down my cheeks like rain, and it seemed as though the entire house was full of the sound of sobbing.

First Uncle gazed at me silently. He looked at my tear-filled eyes, then offered a wan smile. Even as he let me see that smile, he couldn't conceal his bitterness. He said, "Lianyun is gone, and I'm desperately lonely. That's why I've come to see you." Then, he held up the bowl of hard-boiled eggs. He didn't eat, but merely held the bowl in his hands. He said, "Lianyun has left us. You shouldn't be heartbroken. This is her fate. It was her fate to be taken from us at such a tender age."

After a while, First Uncle added, "Perhaps it's just as well, since in the end life is a punishment, bringing endless suffering and endless pain." At this moment, First Uncle also began weeping. His tears poured into the bowl of hard-boiled eggs that I had just prepared for him, like rain pouring off a roof onto the earth below.

I handed him a towel to wipe away his tears, and said, "It's almost dark. First Uncle, would you like to eat something?"

He wiped his tears, and replied, "Sure, let's eat something."

That day my wife happened to have taken our son to see her mother, leaving me alone at home. I didn't know how to cook, so when my wife wasn't home I usually just ate instant noodles. Naturally, I couldn't serve First Uncle instant noodles, so I opened the refrigerator and found some steamed rice my wife had left me. I cooked First Uncle a scrambled egg with rice, and a pot of so-called three-delicacies soup. When I served him the scrambled eggs and the soup, I was racked by an acute sense of guilt, feeling that I should take him into the city to have a good meal. But by that point it was already dark, and our eyes were completely bloodshot. Plus, I didn't want to go back to the barracks and have someone notice we had been crying and ask us what was wrong. So I had no choice but to prepare something to eat at home.

My wife didn't return that evening, so First Uncle and I chatted deep into the night. Mostly, it was First Uncle who did the talking, as I sat and listened. I listened as he talked about his brothers and about me and my cousins. He talked about his father's generation—which is to say, my grandfather's generation. I don't remember most of what he told me or what the point of it was. But what I do remember is that First Uncle spoke very fluently, as though he were telling me everything that had been pent up in his heart from the first half of his life.

We didn't fall asleep until very late.

First Uncle got up the next morning. As he was waking up, I went out to buy some soy milk and fried dough sticks. I also went to ask my supervisor for the day off, since I planned to take First Uncle to the old capital of Kaifeng to look around. But after First Uncle finished his breakfast, he announced that he wanted to return home. He said that he had already been to Kaifeng two years earlier, and that he wasn't interested in returning now. He said that this time he had come to Kaifeng simply in order to talk to me. He said that after chatting the previous night, he felt more relaxed than he had been in two years.

He said that now that he was relaxed, he wanted to return home. Furthermore, as soon as he mentioned wanting to return home, he immediately had a strong urge to board a train or a long-distance bus.

I had no choice but to let him return home.

I quickly prepared a travel pack with some fruit and clothing he could take with him. I remembered how every winter First Uncle never had warm shoes to wear, so I asked a friend who managed the army warehouse to help find me a pair of cotton boots; then I went to the warehouse and asked the supervisor to sign a permission form allowing me to buy them. I gave First Uncle seventy or eighty yuan as spending money, and then I went down to the long-distance bus station to buy him a ticket. But when I took First Uncle to the bus station to see him off, he said something that, to this day, still gives me a bittersweet feeling. Just as he was leaving, he smiled and told me that the egg and rice dish that I had prepared for him was delicious and that it was the best he had had in his entire life. He said that the next time he came to Kaifeng, this would be the only thing he would eat.

13. RESTING

First Uncle never returned to Kaifeng.

He never again had my scrambled eggs and rice.

He never again left our family's village.

Over time, First Uncle's children—my cousins—all got married and established their own families. They resembled a nursery full of saplings, and as soon as the saplings grew into trees they were transplanted so that they could face the sun and the rain and enjoy their own destinies. Meanwhile, First Uncle's life was such that, after his children grew up and reached maturity, he had to take their destiny, like a mysterious leather-bound book, and place it in their hands.

One after another, all of his children left his household and established their own families.

One after another, each moved into a new tile-roofed house and courtyard.

By the time the ninth nephew on my father's side of the family had gotten married, First Uncle had already completed his primary objective in this life, which was to ensure that all of his children were able to establish their own families. My cousin Facheng, because he was the eldest of First Uncle's children, had shouldered a larger share of the burden of helping his parents and his siblings. He assumed this responsibility without complaint. He initially trained to be a craftsman, and subsequently taught himself design and management, permitting him to establish a village construction team in which his siblings and cousins could work as craftsmen. Although this was exhausting work, it nevertheless gave our clan a chance to make a bit of profit. It enabled us, despite the difficulty of our lives, to have some money to cover household expenses, and even have a little left over. More importantly, unlike poorer villagers who had to continue going out to the fields every day and enduring backbreaking labor even into their sixties or seventies, simply to afford basic necessities like oil, salt, vinegar, and soy sauce, First Uncle could afford to rest when he reached the age when one should rest.

During the slack season, First Uncle would wander around the village, and on winter nights he would sit next to the stove and watch television. He was able to enjoy that idle life that the elderly deserve. Once, when I returned home from a business trip, he smiled at me and said he was enjoying a good life—his children were all filial and would periodically send him money; he didn't need to work, but also didn't need to worry about having enough to eat or wear. He said this on a snowy day, when he was sitting in front of the television, though he wasn't watching it. He placed his hand next to the stove, and I saw that he was wearing the wool military boots I had bought him. He told me that he didn't even have words to describe how warm those boots were, and when he wore them he wouldn't feel cold, no matter where he went. He smiled and added that he didn't need to worry about having enough to eat or wear, but still couldn't forget how tasty he found that scrambled egg and rice dish I had fixed for him.

I wished First Uncle could have had a chance to travel. I wished he could have gone to wander around the city. Of course, I said with a smile, if I had a chance, I'd have my wife—his niece—cook him a tasty dish of scrambled eggs and rice, because I had learned to cook from her.

First Uncle and I agreed that he would return to Kaifeng the following spring, and I would take him to the location of the former capital of the Song dynasty and treat him to several meals cooked by my wife. However, the following spring, he didn't return.

The following summer, he didn't return either.

In fact, he never returned.

Instead, he became paralyzed.

He suffered an aneurysm, and although his condition was stabilized, it became difficult for him to move around. Each winter he would sit in the sun in front of his entryway, and each summer he would sit in the gatehouse passageway in front of his tile-roofed house. Society had changed a lot, and by this time, peasants' lives were much brighter than before. My father's generation struggled tirelessly for food, clothing, and housing. They struggled to build their sons their own three-room, tile-roofed houses. But now, those adobe-roofed and tile-roofed houses have gone out of style—like trees that become old and shriveled before they have a chance to become fully grown. Those houses were like children of fallen aristocrats, standing in a modern city, recalling their former lives. When people from our village started building new houses twenty years ago, they began by pursuing traditional tile and brick houses, after which they moved on to multistory structures. Now, however, no one talks about simply "building houses"; instead they use more refined terms like *construction* and *architecture*. Furthermore, they began pursuing the architectural styles found in the city. Although every era's long march begins in the countryside, cities quickly jump to the front of the procession. Nevertheless, this sort of pursuit of what is considered civilized continues burning in the hearts of villagers, and one could say that they may have viewed some of our village hovels as potential sites of new architecture. That three-room tile-roofed house that First Uncle painstakingly built with his own flesh and blood ended up like a memory buried in the weeds of time. For First Uncle, it was like a stone monument to his life.

That house had been an eyewitness to the most exhausting and arduous period of my uncle's life.

By that point, however, the house was already uninhabited, but when First Uncle wasn't sitting in front of it warming himself in the sun on a cold day, he was instead back in the passageway cooling off on a hot day. It was almost as if his lifetime of hard work building the house had simply been so that it could be there for him in his old age—keeping him company, with his wheelchair, crutches, and loneliness.

14. FUNERAL AFFAIRS

It was Mother who, in a long-distance phone call in the early 1990s, gave me the news that First Uncle had become paralyzed.

When I returned to our family home, I entered the village and saw First Uncle sitting alone under a tree in front of his house, with his crutches by his side. Because First Uncle was constantly drooling, a family member had sewn a handkerchief onto his shirt so that he could more conveniently wipe his hands and his face—the same way that you might tie a handkerchief onto the front of a child's shirt. The moment I saw him sitting there all alone, my heart lurched, and

I almost burst into tears. At that moment, I exclaimed to myself, "Life . . . ah, life!"

When First Uncle saw me, he appeared as excited as always, and flashed me a radiant smile. When he attempted to move, I ran up and stopped him. I handed him the gifts that I had brought him, placing them on his lap, but First Uncle suddenly said, "I hear you are being transferred to Beijing?"

I nodded.

First Uncle was silent for a while, then remarked that if my transfer to Beijing was so that I could be promoted and become an official, then it made sense, but if it wasn't, then there was no need to be transferred to a location farther from home. He pointed out that my father had already passed away, leaving my mother alone in our family house, and suggested that I should be posted somewhere closer to home and focus on looking after my mother. Then, he urged me to quickly return home, saying that my mother was waiting for me. It was during that trip that I decided to prepare First Uncle a bowl of scrambled eggs and rice. But as I was planning this with my mother, she pointed out that after First Uncle had fallen ill, he preferred eating the sort of roasted sweet potatoes that you can buy in the street. She said that when her sister-in-law returned from the county seat, she would often bring First Uncle some roasted sweet potatoes she had bought in the city. The potatoes were sweet, fragrant, and golden red, and First Uncle said these were the good kind. Mother said that all of First Uncle's children, nieces and nephews, and their spouses were all very filial toward him, buying him food and clothing, and making every effort to prevent his suffering. She said there were several other villagers who had suffered strokes, but most of them passed away quickly, and even those who managed to survive partially paralyzed were usually far worse off than First Uncle.

First Uncle, on the other hand, was able to enjoy a certain amount of freedom, move around, and chat with people. Mother repeatedly said that his children and their spouses were very filial and attentive, and the problem was that just when First Uncle reached the age when he should be enjoying happiness, he happened to fall ill. Before I had to return to the army, I went to see First Uncle again, and he discussed his life with me.

First Uncle said, "Lianke, I'm afraid I don't have much longer to live."

I said, "How is that possible?"

First Uncle said, "I'm not afraid to die. Your father died several years ago and is waiting for me, so when I arrive I won't be lonely. There are also your cousins Tiecheng and Lianyun. I often dream about them."

I said, "First Uncle, you mustn't think about these things."

First Uncle laughed; then he moved his crutch from one side of his body to the other. He resembled a child who wants something but is too embarrassed to ask for it, yet at the same time seemed proud and emboldened by that desire. He said that he had already told Facheng and my other cousins that his entire life he wanted to flaunt his wealth. Regardless of how poor he might be, he still wanted to build them houses; and when they got married, he always wanted to invite lots of guests and feed them well. He said that in his village, for all the weddings and funerals he had personally handled, he would invariably pull out all the stops. Even when someone in someone else's family died, he would regard them with disdain if their funereal caps and clothing were too small. He said he hoped that when he died, his daughters and nieces would make sure that his funeral would feature many more paper lanterns and traditional performances than usual.

He said that when a villager died, there were generally a handful of filial mourners, or at most a few dozen. When he died, however, because his was a large clan, he hoped that we would organize all of his descendants so that he might have a funeral procession consisting of more than a hundred filial mourners.

He requested that the music be performed by the best musicians, and that they should invite at least two musical troupes, so that when one got tired the other could step in. And when neither troupe was tired, and there were many guests, the two troupes could play together.

First Uncle shared with me his wishes for his funeral, even specifying his desires for the coffin, funeral attire, paper lanterns, traditional performances, and so forth. Everything that he might need for the afterlife, he arranged in advance for my siblings and cousins to take care of. Meanwhile, my only assignment was to make sure—in the event that he were to pass away suddenly—that I not be so far away that I would not be able to make it back in time to attend.

I laughed.

I told him, "When that day arrives, even if I happen to be on the other side of the earth, I'll definitely still make it back."

Reassured, First Uncle nodded, as though now that the arrangements were complete, he could calmly depart. But after making these arrangements, he suddenly thought of something, and asked me, "When you return after I die, will your wife, little Li, also be able to make it back?"

I replied, "Of course."

First Uncle said skeptically, "But she's an 'outsider' (which is to say, someone from outside the village), so if she doesn't return, what will you do?"

I laughed, and said, "If she doesn't return for the funeral, I'll simply divorce her."

First Uncle also laughed.

First Uncle's satisfied laugh seemed to suggest that now that he had finalized all of his arrangements, the only thing left was for him to peacefully sit there waiting for death to arrive—waiting for that final moment of life either to amble over or to suddenly appear before him. It was as if life and death took the form of a visible time and tangible material, approaching him step-by-step. It was as if, sitting under a tree, he were to look up and see a yellow leaf fluttering down from the tree. There was no wind or rain, just a stillness and warmth. There was a warm sunlight surrounding that leaf, leaving it in a peaceful and beautiful state. Because of its shape, the leaf fluttered slowly through the air, turning and spinning as it fell to the earth. At some location on the ground, in that life-filled spot, there was First Uncle's body and his gaze. His gaze was fixed on that location, and he watched as that yellow leaf swirled around in the air. This would turn out to be his last breath and moment of final peace, the most serene and tranquil moment of his life. As soon as the leaf hit the ground, First Uncle's life would end. First Uncle was not afraid of the leaf's falling or of death, and he sat there quietly waiting for the leaf to land and for the end that it would herald. It was as if he understood that life's endless toil and fatigue, rushing about and cycling around, was in the end all for the sake of this final moment—for death and oblivion.

First Uncle's tranquility in the face of death filled me with wonder and admiration.

First Uncle had never discussed his understanding of the relationship between life and death, but I was convinced that thanks to his recognition of death, he had a new understanding of life. First Uncle couldn't read, and perhaps it was precisely on account of his inability to read that there had been no need for him to elevate life and death to the philosophical level of intellectuals. Perhaps it was precisely on account of the fact that he couldn't read that there was no need for him to experience agony and despair after reading something in a book. If he had been able to read, he might have felt a sense of helplessness and panic when faced with the inevitability of old age, infirmity, and death, and he might have let out a silent trembling cry of sorrow. Perhaps it was precisely on account of the fact that First Uncle was an illiterate peasant and, like everyone else from the countryside, was to a greater or lesser extent superstitious and believed in the afterlife, that he was therefore able to face death with such calmness. I thought, even if First Uncle didn't believe in the afterlife, he certainly must have believed that human life has an origin and a destination. Therefore, it was precisely in the face of death that First Uncle could display this calmness and imperturbability, this peacefulness and self-sufficiency—that he could have such a secular yet transcendent sense of renewal and purpose in the face of life's road and homeward journey.

Yes, First Uncle definitely believed that each life has its destination.

It was precisely because First Uncle believed that each life has its own destination that he was able to show such a preternatural sense of calm. Even Buddhism's understanding of the relationship between life and death is driven by a superstitious belief in reincarnation. This is religion's way of alleviating the anxieties that people have in the face of death and represents the most basic care and respect for life.

I knew First Uncle had no real understanding of Buddhism, Taoism, Christianity, Judaism, or Islam. As soon as he was born on that piece of land, because he had an understanding of "superstition," he therefore had a natural understanding of religion's views on life and death, and his belief in this life and the afterlife, in death and a final destination, gave him an equanimity when facing his own mortality. There are two types of people who are most peaceful in the face of death. The first are real intellectuals, because they are able to fully understand the relationship between life and death and elevate it to the high level of a philosophical problem. When elevated to the level of a philosophical problem, death is no longer so frightening, because death is the birth and proof of philosophy and also the continuation and extension of life. The second are illiterate peasants like First Uncle. They believe in life's origin and destination, and they can understand that death is not a new beginning but rather a process of transference and displacement from one environment to another. Meanwhile, those who are most unhappy in the face of death are those of us who are literate but haven't read many books and have not thought very deeply about these sorts of matters. We are neither able to elevate death to an abstract philosophical problem, nor can we simply believe that death is the transference and displacement of life. We cannot believe that life has its own direction and destination.

In the end, when faced with death, we become like nihilists, and precisely because we have read a few books and understand a few so-called perspectives on life and views on death, our suffering, depression, and enjoyment necessarily lack the peacefulness that First Uncle succeeded in maintaining in the face of death. For a long time—from my youth until I was middle-aged—I had always feared death. Every time I thought of death, I would shiver in terror, secretly shed a tear, and lose interest in everything. After that eye-opening discussion with First Uncle, however, I became calmer in the face of mortality. I don't believe that someone's soul will continue to exist after they pass away, but First Uncle helped me to appreciate that if you can take care of some matters before your demise, it will be possible to lessen the fear associated with death.

15. FACING DEATH

First Uncle passed away in 2006, on the twenty-sixth day of the first month of the lunar calendar.

From the time First Uncle fell ill and began preparing for death, he ended up living another ten years. From the age of seventy-two to eighty-two, First Uncle's life was a continual conversation with death, as life and death mutually reconciled with one another. As far as my siblings and I could recall, eighty-two was a relatively advanced age for someone in our clan. It seemed as though First Uncle should have been able to live even longer, because he was someone who could meet death with equanimity. Based on my observations, for everyone who succeeds in reaching old age, the key reason for their longevity, apart from physiological and medical conditions, is that they are able to treat death as a friend. People who don't fear death but still view death as an enemy will struggle for life, but ultimately they may overextend themselves and deplete their own life. Conversely, people who fear death, even though they may not deplete their own life in the process of struggling for life, may through their fear hasten death's arrival. However, those who are able to treat death as a friend, a colleague, a relative, or even a family member—because they are able to coexist with death, cohabitate with death, speak and converse with death, wake up and go to sleep with death. They will regard death as life's assistant and helper, and as fate's final kith and kin—and precisely because death is near, and because they get along easily with it, these people make it so that death can forget its return route, allowing them to enjoy a little extra time on earth.

I thought that, among the various members of our clan, First Uncle was the one who was able to face death most peacefully. The reason he was able to begin planning his own death so soon was that the pettiness, suffering, and resilience from the preceding two-thirds of his life allowed him, during the final third of his life, to enjoy his children's filial response to his lifetime of suffering. Just as death is like going to the market during the farmer's slack season, elderly peasants in the countryside enter what could be viewed as their life's slack season as they face death, during which they focus only on getting enough to eat, wearing warm clothing, and being surrounded by their family. Because it is the slack season, and because death is simply a process of going to the market or to a relative's house in a neighboring village, there is no need to rest.

I seem to remember reading somewhere that when death invites you to depart from this world, it sends you either a beautiful printed notice or a desolate picture. Even though the letter has already arrived, there is no need to open the envelope immediately and see the date and message. Instead, it is enough to know that it has arrived, and you can then place the notice on a table or at the head of your bed. Alternatively, you could place it inside one of the books on your bookshelf or behind one of those large red-and-green calendars you often find in rural houses. Afterward, you can continue doing what you normally would—carrying an umbrella when it rains and a fan when it is sunny, and not letting the arrival of that notice change your daily routine in the slightest. As long as you remember this, the notice will no longer have any significance, even after you forget the date of death's arrival, and then it will not matter that death may stop sending new notices and instead may knock on your door in person.

When death comes knocking, you mustn't become flustered or anxious, and you mustn't start yelling or cursing, the way you might treat an enemy or an unwelcome guest. Instead, you should simply invite death in. You should ask it to come over to the table or bed, and treat it courteously and warmly. You should chat and drink tea together. That way, it is possible that death—which originally was going to escort you away—might even forget why it came knocking in the first place.

In this way, you may reach an advanced age, and you may be able to retrieve several days, months, years, or even decades of life and happiness from death's grasp.

From the trajectory of First Uncle's illness and the last decade of his life, I'm unable to determine whether or not he knew the secret of interacting with death, but he nevertheless proved one important point: it was precisely his calm conversation with death that enabled him to remain in stable health despite his chronic illness. And it is also because he (knowingly or unknowingly) stumbled upon this fact without committing it to memory, that at the age of eighty-two he could ignore the reality that death was perpetually by his side. He forgot that death existed, and forgot that death was constantly following him, day and night.

In the end, however, death finally came to its senses and whisked him away.

16. DESTINATION

One winter when First Uncle was warming himself by the fire, he got up to add more kindling, whereupon he suddenly fell, and he passed away soon afterward. If he hadn't been warming himself by the fire that day; or if he had remembered that he was sick and had been more careful when he got up to add more kindling; or if he had recalled properly that for the past ten years he had been effectively paralyzed—then maybe he wouldn't have fallen down next to the stove, and his fall wouldn't have jogged death's memory, and in turn this wouldn't have sent him quickly away from this world and his family.

After First Uncle fell, he was taken to the hospital, two *li* away, but before he was even able to make it there, death had whisked him away.

After First Uncle's departure, his children arranged his funeral in accordance with his wishes. They hired two bands comprising musicians of the highest quality and had traditional performances and bought paper lanterns—purchasing so many that there wasn't room for all of them in front of the funeral shed, and they had to place the remainder on either side of the shed. So that all of First Uncle's children would rest easy after his death, during the funeral they also arranged for my cousin Tiecheng to undergo a traditional "ghost wedding," so that they could bury the urn containing Tiecheng's ashes and those of his new bride in the same ancestral grave site.

The day after First Uncle's death, I rushed home. The moon was bright and a winter chill lingered in the air. The entrance to the village was quiet and empty, and in the still night, the light in First Uncle's funeral shed illuminated some dark corners of the living world. Those two nights that I came home for the funeral, I slept on the wheat straw in front of his funeral shed, so that I could keep watch over his soul. In the middle of the night, when everything was quiet, I got up and went to First Uncle's body to change the incense stick that had almost burned down, at which point I heard First Uncle tell me the following things:

He said, "When alive, you mustn't tire yourself out."

He said, "Beijing is far away, and the city is vast. If you become bored or restless while you are there, you should come home frequently."

He said, "When you are young, you should stick close to life. But when you are old, with illness and solitude just around the corner, you should maintain a close relationship with death. You mustn't ever forget that death is always following behind you like a shadow, but you also mustn't constantly be thinking about this."

On the third day after First Uncle's death, all of my siblings and cousins—more than twenty of us—together with all the members of the clan's older generation, totaling over 120 people, formed an impressive funeral procession. Accompanied by loud folk music, we carried First Uncle's body several *li* to the mountain grave site. As we buried the body, I gazed at the pile of fresh earth next to my father's grave. After all the mourners left the grave site, my brothers and I remained in front of that pile of dirt. We lit a fire and ignited a wreath and a paper lantern, and after the flames had died out, in the near-silence of the burned paper fluttering away, I said to First Uncle, "You should wait here. My brothers and I will live well in this world, until one day we will finally come and join you."

CHAPTER 5

Fourth Uncle

1. DAYS AND LIFE

Fourth Uncle left this world last year. He left during the National Day holiday, though I don't know whether he intentionally chose this date to depart. When he passed away he wasn't yet seventy years old and so couldn't really be considered elderly, but neither was he particularly young. When I think back on his life, I rarely consider issues of fate and existence, and instead I choose to focus on his happiness living in our society.

I want to use Fourth Uncle's life to try to better understand the nature of happiness and existence.

People in the city refer to the process of living as "life," while those in the countryside refer to life as the process of "living." While this might appear to involve simply two different terms for the same thing, there is actually a more fundamental difference between the two concepts. "Living" suggests a process of enduring day after day, with each day being the same, and implies a kind of monotony, boredom, hopelessness, and idleness. "Life," on the other hand, conveys a sense of richness, of progress and the future. It has color and vitality and calls to mind the act of walking down a broad road illuminated by bright lights. Although you may never go to a park, enter a library, or swim in a pool, nevertheless libraries, pools, and beautiful (even if abandoned) parks still exist in your life. Life appears to be something that can be changed and improved by people's own will—even if, in practice, this is often not the case. "Living," by contrast, appears to be ossified and unchanging, remaining the same from one generation to the next—even though, in many instances, this is actually not really the case either. Living is an abandoned stone on a mountainside and mindless labor, while life is flowers and trees that have been raised to maturity and that change with the seasons. If living is a blade of grass, then life is a beautiful flower, and if living is a single tree, then life is a verdant park in the center of the city. Of course, vegetation in parks can be easily damaged and abandoned, while stones in a wasteland and trees in the wilderness are much more resilient. When our society considers life, accordingly, it is always careful and meticulous, but when it considers the process of living, it approaches it extravagantly and arbitrarily, chopping away like a hatchet. Life is society's natural-born child, while living is an adoptive stepmother. And if life is a beautiful daughter, beloved by her parents, who always wears florid clothing, then living is a son on whom parents rely but who constantly has to be urged to go out and work, which perhaps is true and appropriate.

We may not be able to say whether living supports and raises life, but let's observe that when a family has only one steamed bun to eat, then, when the parents face their children—which is to say, life and the process of living—they won't simply cut the bun in half and give one half to life and the other half to the process of living. Instead, they divide it into two unequal portions and give two-thirds or even three-quarters to life while leaving the remainder for the ordinary process of living. Similarly, if the parents have only one apple, perhaps they may give the entire thing to life, while giving the process of living only a glass of water.

Given this process of distribution and cultivation, this kind of growth and work, this state of being under the same sun and moon but unable to receive the same sunlight and moonlight, wind and rain—life becomes the happy side of living, while living becomes the boredom and detritus of life. Therefore, life becomes a kind of lightness and enjoyment, beauty and hope, while living becomes a sign of heaviness, boredom, and the meaninglessness and ennui of a cycle in which one day relentlessly follows another.

2. A SHIRT

Fourth Uncle was the first person to help me appreciate the difference between life and living.

Fourth Uncle worked in the Lu Wang Cemetery Cement Factory in Xinxiang. I was always left with a sense of fascination and yearning when I recalled how, every time Fourth Uncle came home to visit his family, he would always take a train from Xinxiang and then transfer to a car. I didn't know how large the cement factory was or what precisely Fourth Uncle did there, nor was I sure whether he was a manager in his own right or was managed by others. But every time he returned home—which was usually once but sometimes twice a year—I always yearned to be able to take a train and car like he did. I envied his uniform, his shirt and pants that were made not from coarse cotton but rather from multi-patterned machine-made cloth—not to mention his leather shoes and nylon socks. When he returned in the summer, he'd be wearing a wide-brimmed sun hat, and when he returned in the winter he'd be wearing white gloves. I was convinced that what he enjoyed could be called life, while what we lived was simply living.

When I was twelve or thirteen, the first book I stole from the shelf at the head of my first sister's bed was a copy of *Journey to the West*, and the second was a foreign urban romance, the title of which I no longer recall. From the latter, which I believe was British, I learned the word *life*, and began to appreciate the difference between life and living. The process of living unfolded in front of me; it could be seen and touched and furthermore was something I experienced every day. The happiness and the mystery of life, by contrast, were like a book whose location I knew but which I was unable to open.

Fourth Uncle was the first page of that book I wanted to open.

Fourth Uncle was also the first page of the happy life for which I yearned.

Previously, like countless other rural children, I had asked Fourth Uncle:

"Are trains very big?"

"Are they very long?"

"How many people can ride on a single train?"

"Is the train's rumbling so loud that, if it is in the mountains, I would be able to hear it from here?"

The first things I knew about trains and the world outside the countryside were all from what Fourth Uncle told me. He explained that in the city, streets were paved with concrete and streetlights burned as bright as fire and stayed on all night, regardless of whether anyone was outside. He also specified the size and wattage of the bulbs, noting that the smallest bulbs were fifteen-watt but produced the same amount of light as one hundred oil lanterns in a single room.

It was as if I knew what the city was like.

It was as if I had already learned to distinguish life from living.

I felt that Fourth Uncle's life was a happy one. As for our own process of living, even if it could be considered happy, it couldn't possibly be compared to Fourth Uncle's life. I wanted to claim some of Fourth Uncle's happiness for ourselves, to supplement our own unhappy process of living—the same way one might reroute water from a river in order to irrigate a dry field. From these days of longing, I gradually grew up, moving from elementary school to middle school. Eventually, in the summer of that year, as I was longing for Fourth Uncle's return, I saw him arrive wearing a white shirt with blue stripes. The shirt's fabric was not handwoven cloth nor was it machine-made cloth, but rather it was a kind of exquisite, shiny polyester.

All the villagers tugged at his shirt and asked, "What kind of fabric is this?"

Fourth Uncle replied, "It's polyester."

The villagers responded to seeing something they had previously only ever heard of—a new product that was currently popular in the city. They crowded around Fourth Uncle, expressing their envy for the city and their disgust for the countryside.

I stood at a distance. I knew that the shirt was not just a shirt but also a happy life.

I yearned to have that sort of happy life.

I was bursting with excitement after the other villagers left Fourth Uncle's home, and as Fourth Uncle was going inside, I went up to him and abruptly asked: "Uncle, why don't you give me your shirt?"

Fourth Uncle was clearly surprised by this request. He stood there staring at me, and seemed to be debating how to respond—when suddenly, either as a reflex or out of a stroke of inspiration, I blushed and added, "Let me wear it. I'm already our class monitor at school."

Fourth Uncle didn't say a word. Without further hesitation, he promptly removed his shirt, folded it, wrapped it in an old newspaper, and stuffed it into my hands. Then he patted my head with his large hand, the way that First Uncle, after giving me a piece of candy, used to do. With this, the shirt became mine. Because of those pieces of candy and that shirt, now, more than thirty years later, I can still feel the warmth and love of First Uncle's and Fourth Uncle's hands patting me on the head—like the light of a never-setting sun shining down on my head, body, and heart.

When I went to school that afternoon, I couldn't wait to wear that blue-striped polyester shirt Fourth Uncle had given me. Although as patterned shirts go, it was perhaps not particularly bright and dazzling, if viewed as an ordinary shirt, it was quite colorful and resplendent. On the front it had a row of six silver buttons (our rural shirts, by contrast, had only five buttons, and usually they were made of ordinary cloth), and the buttons gleamed as though made of glittering crystal or moonlight. The shirt had a long and pointed collar, which was stiff and supported my neck, and the shirt seemed to push my waist forward, as though I were the son of a general or emperor heading to school.

When I entered through the middle school's doorway, I felt both shy and proud. Just as I expected, as soon as I stepped through the grape trellis over the door, my classmates immediately stared at me. That day, I was also wearing a pair of plastic sandals my mother had bought me. With the shirt and those sandals and having all the teachers' and students' gazes fixed on me, I experienced an unprecedented feeling of happiness, with life flooding my entire body.

In any event, apart from some female classmates who had urban residency permits and whose parents had national government–issued salaries, none of the other students had ever had a chance to wear polyester clothing. Out of the school's several hundred students, I was the first male student to wear polyester, and out of all the children from the countryside, I was the first to enjoy the happiness of life—like someone who not only sees a peacock for the first time but also manages to obtain one of its feathers.

On that first day, when our language teacher, Zhang, saw me, he stroked my shirt and said with a smile, "This fabric is very shiny. You'll have to study very hard to live up to it."

Our math teacher was a woman whose surname was also Zhang and who happened to be our neighbor. When she came to class, she acted as though she didn't notice I was wearing that garment that caused such great happiness, but after she finished her lesson and assigned us our homework, she stepped down from the lectern, walked over, and then bent down to inspect my collar. Without saying anything about the shirt, she then said, "Work hard. Your math scores are no longer among the top three of the class."

That summer, I wore the polyester shirt that Fourth Uncle had given me to school every day. When the shirt was dirty and needed to be washed, I would always make sure to wash it on a Sunday, so that it would be ready to wear again on Monday.

When Fourth Uncle had to leave at the end of his summer break, I wasn't able to see him off because I had school. When I returned home that evening, Mother told me that Fourth Uncle had returned to his job at the cement factory. She added that before he left, he had removed the *dada* pants he was wearing, then washed and folded them, and left them for me to wear. *Dada* was the term for urea-fertilizer sacks that were imported from Japan, which were made from a kind of chemical fiber with a soft but resilient texture. After the fertilizer was used up, two empty sacks were just enough to make a shirt or a pair of pants. Because that fabric was as soft as silk and continually rustled in the wind, making a *dadada* sound, in the western Henan countryside it was called *dada*. In the early 1970s, that kind of *dada* clothing became popular in China's cities and rural areas, and the Japanese sacks played a very significant role in relieving China's fabric shortages. Unfortunately, several years later, when the Japanese learned that the Chinese were using urea-fertilizer sacks to make clothing, they switched to exporting their fertilizer in the coarse "snakeskin" sacks that are currently ubiquitous in China.

Even later, when the Japanese noticed that, although the Chinese couldn't use the material from snakeskin sacks to make clothing, they could still use it to make gunnysacks and grain sacks, they proceeded to replace the snakeskin sacks with fiberglass ones. Fiberglass, as the name implies, is made from glass fibers, and if your body is in extended contact with it, it will make your skin unbearably itchy. So whenever we see those sacks, we can't help but step back in alarm. When I think back now, it seems that perhaps Japan lacked a sense of empathy for China, but given that we did have that particular history, those urea-fertilizer sacks became embedded in people's memory as a kind of fashion and a symbol of a happy life.

Before Fourth Uncle left me that pair of *dada* pants, he had washed and folded them and then wrapped them in an old newspaper. Mother handed me the parcel, and I opened it and gazed at those pants as though looking at a neatly folded national flag. I felt warm but cautious, and my sense of gratitude to Fourth Uncle was comparable to the sense of solemnity with which I approach the flag.

At that instant, an extravagant desire flashed through my head, as I wondered whether I would ever be able to work in a city like Fourth Uncle and exchange my rural life for a new urban one. It occurred to me that such a future would be so beautiful and happy.

3. QUIET NIGHT

There's something else I should mention.

Fourth Uncle's family also wanted to build a house. They wanted to construct a tile-roofed house, like the one First Uncle's family built at the front of the village. In part, this was because Fourth Uncle's two sons—my cousins Changke and Jianke—would soon be adults, and in part it was because of the salary Fourth Uncle had earned while working in the city, which seemed to have left him significantly better off than those of us who had stayed in the countryside. No matter how much or how little Fourth Uncle was able to earn every month, at least he had a monthly salary.

Because Fourth Uncle had a steady income, to my knowledge he never had to go down to the riverside and haul stones for money, like First Uncle. When Fourth Uncle's family decided to build a house, it's possible they endured endless misery in the process, but only they know for sure. At that time, however, it seemed to me that they built their house more easily than other families. Building a house back then was different from today. Now, you simply need to make sure all the expenses and labor are covered, and the house will come together as easily as water flowing into an irrigation canal. But back then, whenever a family wanted to build a house, or to arrange a wedding or funeral, they always had to worry about economizing. In order to save money, they would make the walls of the house from planks and mud, and for the mud it would be necessary to go collect dirt from a distant field. Society's rural organization system specified that the people's communes should operate on a socialist collective system, with work being carried out by production teams and brigades. Everyone worked tirelessly every day, and for each work point, at most a person could earn a little over ten cents. In their production teams, people could work like dogs for ten hours a day and still earn only eight cents. But to earn these ten cents or so, peasants couldn't afford to skip work and rest. So when villagers or neighbors needed to complete a major task, such as building or repairing a house, they would have no choice but to help each other. Given that they had to work during the day, they would have to carry out this sort of mutual assistance on clear nights, under the light of the moon or the stars.

In order to build his house, Fourth Uncle returned from Xinxiang for half a month. During the day, he would make arrangements for the various tasks involved in the construction process, and at night he would ask other villagers to help haul dirt back from the barren field. Of course, when asking others for help, one cannot afford to shirk in one's own efforts and instead must work even harder than everyone else. After a week, Fourth Uncle was so tired that he collapsed. One moonlit night, Fourth Uncle and I were collecting dirt from that barren field, and after filling the carts we watched as others hauled them away, at which point Fourth Uncle and I sat down on the moonlit field. Tree shadows were swaying back and forth over the earth, clouds were drifting overhead, and a cool autumn breeze was blowing. Crickets were chirping brightly, and their calls echoed through the field. The night was like a poem, and in that poem-like night I told my exhausted uncle several things that I absolutely should not have said.

I remarked, "Life is really pointless."

Fourth Uncle looked up in surprise.

I said, "Working day after day, building houses, and eating—you're exhausted all the time, and only on New Year's are you able to enjoy a good meal."

Fourth Uncle stared at me. "So what do you propose?"

I said, "I don't want to study or work the fields. Instead, I want to get a job, like you." I paused and then added, "As long as I can get out of here, I'll be satisfied."

Fourth Uncle didn't immediately respond. He stared at the village, the houses, the trees, the moonlight, and the starlight in front of us, as though staring at a book, and after looking at several pages, he looked as though he had derived a moral from it, at which point he turned to me and—in a tone that was light and casual, but at the same time very serious—he said, "Lianke, you should treat your parents well. It wasn't easy for them to send you and your siblings to school. One should never forget one's gratitude toward one's parents; because if one does, one's life will have been for nothing." Fourth Uncle picked up his hoe and began trying to break up the ginger stones in the barren field, but after hacking at them a few times, he seemed to feel that our previous conversation had not been completely resolved, so he lifted his hoe toward the moonlit sky, then turned to me and added, "In this world, you can't get a single bowl of good food. If you want to leave home, then wait until you've graduated from middle school, after which you can go and work with me."

During the period when I was in middle school, this was the most solemn thing Fourth Uncle ever said to me. Daily life was so simple and plain, it seemed to be utterly lacking in significance; and even if you extended your thoughts to consider life and fate, they seemed to lack any purpose. But when I remember Fourth Uncle today, his statement that "in this world, you can't get a single bowl of good food" still leaves me extraordinarily depressed. It makes me unable to forget that Fourth Uncle seemed to be living not simply for the sake of "living" but rather in a state that was arbitrarily designated as "happiness." This was absurd and childish—I was like a child who sees a shooting star but then announces he has just discovered a new planet.

Two years later, Fourth Uncle finally completed the house around the time I finished middle school. Given that my own family was living a life like autumn leaves, when Fourth Uncle completed his house my parents finally gave in and let me discontinue my studies and go work with him in the Xinxiang cement factory—so that I could see for myself Fourth Uncle's life—and what I believed to be happiness was combined with an acute sense of embarrassment.

4. AN OCCURRENCE

Fourth Uncle was a so-called shift leader in the loading workshop at the cement factory. The word *shift* in this title refers to the fact that each workshop was divided into three shifts a day, with each shift running for eight hours. Each shift's work—including hauling, transportation, demolition, and mechanical maintenance—was performed collaboratively by several small groups. Fourth Uncle was responsible for one of his workshop's three daily shifts. I initially assumed that a shift leader would be like a production team leader in the countryside, and that after assigning the work to the members of his shift, this leader could simply stand back and watch them work—exchanging hard labor for peaceful rest. In reality, not only did Fourth Uncle need to handle the shift's administrative tasks, he also, whenever one of his workers was out, had to fill in for him. Each of the several dozen workers in every section had one month of vacation time every year, meaning that at any one time at least two or three workers would be away, and therefore Fourth Uncle came to resemble a multiuse screw that would be inserted into a different hole when he went to work each day.

When more than one worker was on vacation and there wasn't enough manpower even with Fourth Uncle's help, he would have to work overtime to make up the difference. Like farming, this work was a form of manual labor and needed to be done without delay.

I once asked Fourth Uncle, "Given that being shift leader is even more laborious than regular work, why do you bother?"

Fourth Uncle replied, "Every day I get an additional thirty cents in pay. Have you forgotten that, back home, I used to be paid only ten cents a day?"

So, that is how it was.

I seemed to have reached a new understanding.

One time their shift had two workers who, in accordance with the prearranged schedule, were on vacation, but in the mechanical maintenance group there was another worker whose mother was ill, and therefore he had to return home to see her, so Fourth Uncle permitted him to take a half month's leave. Since Fourth Uncle had to fill the gaps left by the absent workers, for twenty days in a row he spent several hours working at each of the two posts, to the point that by the time he finally got off work, he'd be so exhausted that he'd go straight to bed without even washing his face. Furthermore, the machinery in the hauling unit often broke down, and when it broke during one shift, workers in the following shift wouldn't be willing to fix it. Given that Fourth Uncle had permitted the worker from the machinery maintenance group to go on leave, he had no choice but to work overtime to cover the worker's responsibilities. One Sunday at the end of a month, I was in my dormitory waiting for Fourth Uncle to get off work and come back to eat. I waited anxiously for more than an hour, but there was no sign of him, so I went to check in his workshop. A cement factory is the dirtiest kind of factory there is, and every square inch was covered in a thick layer of dust and lime. The male factory workers were less concerned about the dust, but the female ones insisted on wearing face masks all day long. Walking down the halls of the factory, you'd see people who didn't even seem human—all wearing black and white work clothes, shiny work helmets with ear guards, and large white face masks that were stained yellow around the nose and mouth area. There was also the sound of machinery in the factory constantly pounding away, every day, sounding like early spring thunderstorms. I walked through this mass of workers getting on and off work, all of whom had their faces partially obscured by face masks. Looking for Fourth Uncle, I reached the workshop in charge of hauling raw materials, which was located on the far side of the factory, next to the mountain's ore vein. When I found him, beneath the stone-crushing machine, I also saw that there were four workers sitting around playing cards while Fourth Uncle was the only person actually performing the repairs.

I looked at the workers and then went underneath that machine, which was as tall as a building, to see Fourth Uncle.

"Why aren't they helping?" I asked.

Fourth Uncle turned. "The machine broke during our shift, and those workers belong to a different one."

I lent Fourth Uncle a hand. "Where are the other machinists from your shift?"

Fourth Uncle laughed. "The one who requested leave had previously offended all his co-workers, so no one was willing to help him out." After this, Fourth Uncle didn't say anything else, and instead he asked me to hand him a wrench and a pair of pliers—like a surgeon asking a nurse for a scalpel. With Fourth Uncle beneath that stone-crushing machine while I stood on its base, the two of us labored for three and a half hours, drenched in grease and the sound of laughter from those workers playing cards, until finally we were able to hand over a functioning machine to the next shift.

In the process of performing the repairs, Fourth Uncle cut his hands and bled profusely. When he emerged from under the machine, we went straight to the clinic, where the doctor gave him several stiches. At the end of the month, Fourth Uncle had his stitches removed and went to the accountant's office to collect his salary, only to discover that his monthly wage had been docked by fifty percent. When he asked why, they replied that when the machinery broke down during his shift, it hadn't been repaired in a timely fashion, and the accident therefore ended up wasting three and a half hours of the next shift's labor. In light of this, they added, Fourth Uncle was getting off lightly by having his salary cut merely by half.

Fourth Uncle laughed bitterly. "Wouldn't it have been possible to *not* dock my salary?"

The official in charge of salaries and penalties looked up at the red slogan on the wall of the accountant's office. Written in Song-style script, the slogan read, SEIZE REVOLUTION, PROMOTE PRODUCTION. After gazing at this slogan for a while, the official turned and gestured for Fourth Uncle to also take a look, and then solemnly declared, "You have undermined not only production but also the revolution. The fact that we are only docking your salary and are not forcing you to write a self-criticism means we are already going easy on you."

After collecting his salary that day, Fourth Uncle had originally planned to take me to a park and a store in Xinxiang. But because his salary had been docked, we didn't go. When I returned to my dormitory, the worker who had gone home to visit his sick mother was waiting in the entranceway. The worker knew that Fourth Uncle's salary had been docked, so he had taken half of his own salary and placed it in an envelope and was determined to leave that envelope in Fourth Uncle's room.

Fourth Uncle asked, "Is your mother doing better?"

The other worker replied, "She's still in the hospital."

Fourth Uncle insisted on returning the envelope with the money to the other man. They began to argue, and after a while Fourth Uncle became angry and said, "Do you think I filled in for you simply in order to earn half of your monthly salary? You may not be a particularly good worker, but you are a filial son, and as soon as you heard that your mother was sick you immediately began to cry, which is why I allowed you to return home."

By this point Fourth Uncle was virtually shouting, which scared the other worker into silence, leaving him standing there with the hand holding the envelope suspended in midair.

When Fourth Uncle saw the other worker stop moving, he lowered his voice and said, "Go home. Your mother is still in the hospital, so take this money to her."

After the worker left, Fourth Uncle still wanted to send his wife some money at the end of the month, as usual. This is because the amount sent, spent, and saved every month was fixed. But that month, in order to send back the usual amount, Fourth Uncle had to borrow money from someone else.

When I observed this situation, my most immediate reaction was that it showed me what kind of person Fourth Uncle really was. Originally, he had occupied a position in my heart that was both vague and clear. My understanding of Fourth Uncle was vague, because I didn't understand him the same way I did Father, First Uncle, and Third Uncle—because for as long as I could remember, Fourth Uncle had always been someone "working away from home," and I could see him only when he returned home to visit. At the same time, my understanding of him was also very clear, because every time he returned home, he would be wearing a clean set of clothes and would bring back many objects and types of food that we couldn't get in the countryside. So, I determined that what we enjoyed at home was the process of living, while what he enjoyed while working away from home was instead life itself.

I had also determined that Fourth Uncle was leading what he viewed as a "happy life."

Now, after working at Fourth Uncle's side and having understood him better, I no longer saw things so simply. In my eyes, his vagueness no longer appeared so vague, and his clarity no longer appeared so clear. With respect to life and living, happiness and sorrow, they continued to cycle back and forth.

5. BOWED-HEADS

Fourth Uncle liked to drink. It seemed as though he was truly happy when, after working for a full day or a full week, he would pack food from the canteen into a takeout container, then return to his dormitory and place it on the table. Next, he would take half a bottle of *baijiu* from the cabinet, and pour some into the cup he used for washing his teeth. Finally, he would take a bite of food and a sip of the *baijiu*. He would close his eyes as he held the porcelain edge of the cup up to his lips; then he would raise his head, carefully tilt the cup, and lightly inhale, and in the process suck the *baijiu* into his mouth. Then he would put the cup down, look around, and hold his breath. In this way, he would savor both the alcohol and his arduous life. When he could not hold his breath any longer, he would slowly swallow the alcohol in his mouth and would then exhale the air he had been holding in his lungs. At this point, his entire body would be relaxed, and it would seem as though all his frustrations had magically disappeared. The true happiness derived from drinking would envelop him.

The *baijiu* was potent and cheap. When it came to drinking, this must have been Fourth Uncle's main principle. The people who usually drank with him were several old workers from the same workshop who had arrived at the factory together. Over time, I discovered that, like Fourth Uncle, those old workers had come from the countryside, leaving their wives and children behind to work the land. They were all what we colloquially referred to as "bowed-heads." When these bowed-heads returned to the countryside, they were regarded as people "who work outside," but when they were "outside," which is to say in the city or the suburbs, the city people, and even the other factory workers, would refer to them as being "from the countryside." It was as though in order to be truly called a worker, a cadre, or a city person, not only did your ancestors have to have been born in the city, at the very least you and your spouse also had to be from the city and earning a salary. Otherwise, if one spouse was working in the city and the other was looking after the house and the land in the countryside, the status of the bowed-head was not merely an identity and a situation, it was also your life and fate.

Bowed-heads are looked down upon in the city because they are attempting to shed their original identity yet are also unable to completely set aside this old identity. They are attempting to obtain a new kind of happiness but are unable to do so. Because of this unrooted identity they are willing to embrace the factory's dirtiest and most exhausting work in order to earn a few extra cents—but then they are mocked for being willing to sacrifice their dignity for the sake of a tiny profit. As a bowed-head, during the busy agricultural harvest season, while other workers go to work according to schedule, you find yourself in a constant state of anxiety—missing your wife and children as well as your parents back home. You worry about the grain that must be harvested, the fields that must be plowed, and the seeds that must be sown. When true city folk hang a calendar behind the door of their dormitory or on the wall of their house, it is so that they can see when Sundays and holidays fall, and they can plan how to spend their free time. But as for you bowed-heads, you don't put this sort of vulgar calendar up on the wall but instead place a solemn desk calendar on your table. Even if every page of that desk calendar contains Tang and Song dynasty poems, its primary use will still be to remind you which is the current solar term. During the busy agricultural season, you always have to figure out a way to return to the countryside—because if you don't, an avalanche of letters from your wife and parents will arrive at your doorstep, screaming your name.

The temporality of bowed-heads is neither that of living nor that of life. Instead, it is a temporality in which not only is the process of living filled with exhaustion and frustration but life itself also periodically has moments of happiness and bliss. If we mention bowed-heads today, it is as if we are referring to an outdated term or a word in some local dialect. But at that time, the term *bowed-head* referred to a class that could be found in every city, factory, and department in China. It was a special fate and unique way of life. Their most notable characteristic is that they are very industrious while at work, because they are afraid that if they are careless they may lose their livelihood. But during the busy agricultural season they have no choice but to return home, where they are treated with respect but still need to throw themselves into their work—in order to squeeze an entire year's labor into a single month. There is one more thing that must be mentioned, which is that when these bowed-heads get off work at the factory, they frequently get together to drink and enjoy the sort of happiness and bliss they couldn't enjoy in the countryside.

And that is how Fourth Uncle started to drink.

It seemed that all the bowed-heads in their factory drank and acted as though they would be betraying themselves if they didn't drink. Sometimes they drank alone, and sometimes they drank together. And it was when they drank that I was able to discover some details about their lives—such as the fact that they were mostly bachelors who had to endure the frustrations of both the countryside and the city. Because of these frustrations, whenever they had free time they would gather together and eat and drink. Whenever they could find an opportunity to drink, they would approach it the same way they did their factory work—arriving punctually, drinking merrily, and playing drinking games until one of them eventually got too drunk or passed out.

Fortunately, although Fourth Uncle liked to drink, he rarely drank to excess. Half a year after I went to work with Fourth Uncle, there was one occasion when the younger brother of one of the workers in his workshop was going to get married. Although this worker was also a bowed-head, his family was from the outskirts of Xinxiang, not far from the cement factory. He invited his co-workers to attend the wedding, and so they all planned to go to his hometown to drink.

Fourth Uncle began making preparations early on. A month before the wedding, he went into the city to buy the worker a cashmere blanket and, in order to appear generous, half a month before the wedding, he took some of the factory's cotton gloves that he had saved up, unthreaded them, then took the rolls of thread to a store near the factory and exchanged them for a patterned tablecloth. After that, all he had to do was wait for the day of the wedding, at which point he would ride his bicycle several dozen *li* to attend the ceremony and drink.

On the Sunday of the wedding, the workmates assembled early to go out together. They were all neatly dressed and in high spirits. They polished their bikes—or the bikes they had borrowed—until they gleamed, and it almost seemed as though they themselves were the ones who were getting married.

However, when the group set out, Fourth Uncle didn't go with them. Explaining that he had something he needed to do, he told them to leave first.

By ten that morning, Fourth Uncle still hadn't left.

At ten thirty, Fourth Uncle stepped outside and peered up at the sky. He stood there for a while but ended up remaining in his dormitory.

I realized that Fourth Uncle must have encountered some sort of difficulty, because otherwise he would have already left. Guests needed to arrive before noon, and this was particularly true for Fourth Uncle, since like his co-workers, he enjoyed festive occasions where he might find some bliss in alcohol. That week, I had worked seven night shifts in a row, and so, on Sunday, I happened to be home during the day. I initially assumed that the reason Fourth Uncle hadn't left yet was that he didn't have enough money, so I took my own salary for the month and placed it on the table in front of him.

Fourth Uncle smiled bitterly and then shook his head.

Confused, I stared at him.

Fourth Uncle once again smiled at me, then looked up at the white polyester shirt hanging on the clothesline outside, and said softly, "I washed it yesterday, but it isn't dry yet."

I turned and looked outside and saw that his white shirt and a set of work clothes were hanging from a washing line he had fashioned out of metal wire. Through the washing and the trees, I could see that the windless sky was overcast and still. The sound of machinery from the factory behind the dormitory resonated like boulders rolling down a mountain. It was at that moment that I came to appreciate Fourth Uncle's happiness and his embarrassment over his condition— as though I had suddenly glimpsed the disorderly mess behind the great, resplendent door of his life. It was as if I had walked through a dilapidated gateway into a locked flower garden, and was greeted by a scene of desolation and decay. After a brief hesitation, I went to another building, where there were three temporary dormitory rooms, and grabbed the blue-striped polyester shirt that Fourth Uncle had given me several years earlier. The collar was somewhat frayed, but the shirt was clean and neatly folded—like a book full of stories.

When I handed the shirt to Fourth Uncle, he smiled at me. That smile was thin and tight, like an autumn leaf drifting through the air. That day, a depressed Fourth Uncle put on the shirt that he had taken off and given me three years earlier, and which I was now returning to him, neatly folded. That was how he went to attend the wedding. He went to drink those wedding libations he had been anticipating for so long. As he disappeared down the cement road in front of the dormitory, he resembled a speck of dirt from the countryside that had somehow come to land on a dust-covered road in the outskirts of the city.

That day, Fourth Uncle got drunk.

After he returned in the middle of the night, he suddenly began bawling and kept repeating the same thing: "How can life be so hard?! How can it be so hard?!" As he said this, it felt like he was driving a nail into my heart. After pouring him several cups of water, I was eventually able to calm him down and get him to bed. The next day, he got up when I was still asleep, then woke me up and asked me to go with him to a department store in Xinxiang, explaining that he wanted to buy new sets of clothes for me, my cousin Shucheng, and himself. He said that without embracing risk, one cannot survive; and that as long as we liked something, we would buy it, regardless of how expensive it might be. In the end I convinced him not to go, but as he was saying that he should embrace risk and buy everyone a new set of clothing, he had a bright and confident smile on his face, as though he had found true happiness.

6. AFTER THE HARVEST

When the wheat ripened, Fourth Uncle returned home to spend half a month harvesting the grain.

I don't know how miserable he was when he returned home that year, but I'm sure his misery definitely couldn't compare with that of those people who were working the land full-time. I remember how every year during the harvest season, regardless of whether or not Fourth Uncle was able to make it back to the countryside, Father and First Uncle would always urge me and my siblings, together with First Uncle's own children, to go to Fourth Uncle's house and help Fourth Aunt harvest the grain. At the time, Fourth Uncle's children were still young, but my cousins Changke and Jianke began going out into the fields when they were just a few years old. They would work in the wheat fields in summer and the millet fields in the fall, to harvest grain and dig irrigation canals. Even though they were still young, there wasn't anything they didn't help with, and thus they led much more difficult lives than children in the city. Today, they already have their own families and are parents in their own right—but the fact that they came to understand the world and to shoulder many of life's complexities at such a young age is surely related to their bowed-head family background. But precisely because they began working like adults while still very young—taking a sharp scythe and proceeding into the fields, with the hot sun shining down on their heads like a furnace, like lambs who had just learned to walk and were immediately faced with the blazing sun—I frequently wondered whether Fourth Uncle had fully carried out his duties as a father. One year, Fourth Uncle did not return for the summer harvest, and when I went to help his family I became so exhausted I could barely stand up. I began to suspect that the reason Fourth Uncle avoided returning home during the busy agricultural season was that he was averse to physical labor. That summer, my cousin Changke harvested wheat and took it to the threshing ground, where he threshed it and left it to dry in the sun. As a teenager, he had to do work that men from the countryside normally don't do until they are in their thirties. Meanwhile, Jianke, who was even younger, while harvesting the wheat was poked by thorns that made him unbearably itchy, and soon his body was covered in bloody scratches. After we finally managed to finish harvesting the wheat and left the stalks bundled together at the front of the field, Jianke suddenly disappeared. From morning till night, he didn't return home to eat, nor did he go to the usual places to play. We looked for him everywhere, until in the middle of the night we found him on a pile of wheat stalks. When we found him, he rubbed his eyes and asked, "Why did you wake me up? I'd just fallen asleep!"

That year, Jianke was only eleven or twelve years old.

In the north, the summer wheat harvest season is a road that all local bowed-head workers must walk down. In the summer of the year I went to join Fourth Uncle to work in the cement factory, he returned to harvest the wheat as usual, and as usual, after he went back to the factory, he promptly fell into a deep sleep. When he saw that I had returned to the dormitory from the mines, he invited me to go with him to take a bath. The cement factory had many limitations, but it had one thing that made people truly happy—it offered free baths. The water in the showers was hot and abundant, and at the turn of the faucet, it would flow over your body like a soft stone. Furthermore, there were many faucets and bathing pools, and when you wanted a bath you never had to wait. When you walked into that garage-like bathing hall, you would often notice you were the only one there. This was especially true of the middle pool, which was boiling hot and, apart from an occasional old man, usually empty. On that particular day, I went with Fourth Uncle to soak in that middle pool. Because a bath relieves fatigue, Fourth Uncle and I both took a deep breath and slowly exhaled—as though in that instant we were both seized by the happiness and good spirit we had long been pursuing. The pools were each as large as a three-room house, and at the narrowest they were still five or six meters wide. Separated by a distance of five or six meters, Fourth Uncle and I sat naked on opposite sides of one pool. Between us were clouds of steam that were so large we couldn't even see each other clearly. Then I said something that anyone nearby could have heard.

I said, "Uncle, is your family's wheat doing well this year?"

"Yes . . ." Fourth Uncle said. "Yes, it is. At harvest time, all the workers developed blisters on their hands. But when the work points were assigned a monetary value, each work point was worth only twelve cents."

Twelve cents. I mean, if I were to pick up two tattered leather cement sacks from the side of the road in front of the cement factory and sell them to the recycling center in the entrance, I could earn as much money as a peasant who has slaved away in the fields all day—even a peasant who has worked like a horse or ox for days during the busy summer. I stared at the damp fog in front of me and also looked through it at Fourth Uncle. I followed up on Fourth

Uncle's statement by remarking, "At home working the land, one is truly like a horse or ox!"

Fourth Uncle reflected for a moment, then replied, "At home, there are always periods of the year when the workload is lighter, but when you are working away from home there are no slack periods." After shifting the topic in this way, Fourth Uncle proceeded to discuss which was better: working at home or outside. Naturally, he concluded that if people working away from home can find work that is clean, dignified, and relaxing, then they will come to have some power and dignity, and they may find a spouse in the city, thereby becoming bona fide urban residents. But if you end up in a filthy and exhausting location like a cement factory or coal pit, then you will neither advance nor regress. If you try to marry a young woman from the city, she will resent you for being too poor, and if you try to marry another worker like yourself, you'll find that they all have their sights set on cadres, or at least workers with a higher status. So you'll have no choice but to return to a rural family and become a bowed-head, and then you'll have no choice but to resolve yourself to staying at home and working the land.

Although Fourth Uncle's personal experiences might appear to have been simple and basic, they contained a sweetness and bitterness that people who have not had similar experiences will never be able to comprehend. As he was telling me all this, he had already finished his bath and was sitting on the edge of the pool, letting the hot water soften his calluses and his tough skin. He was in the process of lancing the blood blisters on his hands with a small pair of scissors he had brought with him. Blood flowed from his palm and down his fingertips, and after it was diluted in the pool's hot water, the dark red blood became light pink. It became even lighter as it flowed toward the edge of the pool and then into the pool itself. As he was speaking, I went over and massaged Fourth

Uncle's shoulders, then sat down beside him. I watched his peaceful expression and how every time he popped a blister he would wave his hand, but I didn't really understand the significance of his discussion of who was happier: those people "working on the outside" or country folk.

Only many years later, when I was in the army and was promoted to cadre, and when I was trying to find a wife and was determined to find a city girl, did I feel a belated understanding of what Fourth Uncle had been trying to tell me. I finally realized the effect that his comments had had on me. I don't know whether my current life should be called life or living, but I must acknowledge that my understanding and my pursuit of life and living at that time were not unconnected to Fourth Uncle's own life. Even if my understanding of life and living was misguided, or even completely wrong, it nevertheless came to function as an article of faith, a rough worldview. During my youth, this understanding provided a basic support for my struggle and efforts.

When Fourth Uncle retired, he didn't hand over his job in Xinxiang to either of his two sons but rather to his daughter, Suping. This decision constituted a major breach of the rural tradition of prioritizing sons over daughters. At the time, none of Fourth Uncle's fellow villagers could understand his choice, and even his own children were bewildered. I think he made this decision because the hardship he had endured convinced him that you must either resolve yourself to becoming a complete peasant or else you must attempt to become a complete city person—because when you are half-rural and half-urban, you not only don't have access to what peasants perceive as the happiness and the job of urban life, you also don't have access to what city dwellers perceive as the leisure and freedom of rural life. Instead, all you have are the sorts of frustrations and insecurities that city dwellers and country folk both share.

To tell the truth, to this day I cannot say with certainty how Fourth Uncle understood family and existence, city and countryside, life and living. But I sense that he hoped his children and I would either become full-fledged peasants who worked the soil from dawn to dusk, or else that we would make every effort to become full-fledged city residents and try to minimize our interaction with the land and the countryside. Precisely because he had this wish, by 1977 I was already working like an old peasant in the cement factory but would periodically return to the countryside to sow the fields and for the harvest. I performed backbreaking labor every day for six hours, and continued in this way for several dozen days. This confirmed to me that life was indeed like a dark cave or a bottomless well.

One day, Fourth Uncle suddenly came up the mountain to bring me a telegram instructing me to return home immediately upon receipt of the message. With considerable anxiety, I walked down the mountain and to the city. With Fourth Uncle, I went to the post office and spent over an hour arranging to call my family long-distance to ask them what had happened. It turned out that the reason I was being summoned was that the year was 1977—not 1976 and even less 1975, 1974, or 1973. The year 1977 was significant because this was when China's national university entrance exams were reinstituted. As long as you were Chinese, regardless of whether you had graduated from high school, middle school, or even only elementary school—if you wanted to you could go to a testing site and take the test to get into university and test your fate.

That afternoon before dusk, Fourth Uncle hurriedly bought me a train ticket, helped me pack, and even gave me a couple of large apples to eat on the train. I estimate I had spent a total of just around two years doing piecework with him, but when I suddenly had to leave, I felt as though I were bidding goodbye to the father who had raised me since birth. The train left in the middle of the night, meaning that there was some time between dinner and when I had to go catch the train—time I would savor like half a bowl of hot, nourishing soup that you can't bear to finish. In the factory, workers typically ate dinner early, and the sun would still be high in the sky when they finished. So Fourth Uncle and I, together with my cousin Shucheng, all sat quietly in the room, while rays from the setting sun shone in through the window and illuminated the table and floor. The air in the room smelled of moisture and laundry detergent mixing with the odor of the food we had brought back from the canteen but hadn't yet finished. In those days, the flavor of life and the taste of daily life mixed together like dirty water, and my uncle, my cousin, and I were immersed in this mortal mixture. It was like sunlight on a winter morning, which gently warms the trees and plants out in the fields that had been frozen all winter, until the sun disappears behind the buildings on the western side of the city. When the sound of the train horn cut through the silence, causing the window glass and window paper to tremble, I knew it was time for me to head out. I had to go seek a different kind of life. As Fourth Uncle and Shucheng prepared to send me on my way, Fourth Uncle grabbed my bag and said, "It's time to go. I want you to take the exam, and do well."

I gave my uncle and my cousin a bitter smile, and said, "I'm afraid I probably won't, given that I didn't even finish the second year of high school."

Fourth Uncle said, "If you don't pass the exam, you can always come back here and continue doing piecework with me. If you do pass, however, you'll never again need to lead the kind of life that your parents and fourth uncle have had to lead."

Shucheng then took my bag from Fourth Uncle, and we left. Fourth Uncle came out last, and with a bang he locked the door's black steel lock—as though cutting off my retreat and encouraging me to struggle forward in a new direction.

7. IN THE RAIL STATION

By contemporary standards, the Xinxiang rail station could not be considered luxurious or modern, much less luxuriously modern. Located at a considerable distance from the city center, the station's waiting area was like an empty warehouse, and while some of the iron and wood waiting chairs were still in good condition, others were in various states of disrepair, with broken legs or missing backrests. Fourth Uncle, Shucheng, and I sat there for a while, whereupon Fourth Uncle went to buy me a packet of crackers to eat on the train. Then I got up—both because I was afraid I might miss the train and also because I wanted to be one of the first ones on, so I might be able to get a seat and nap on the journey.

The train station was as cold and empty as a barren field, but the tracks stretched into the night like a pair of fried dough sticks. The platforms beneath every pair of tracks were made from cement blocks, and their worn edges resembled a collapsed ridge around a field. The moon was in its crescent phase, though I can't remember whether it was waxing or waning. All I remember is that it was bright and hazy. It moved at a constant speed, and sometimes it was behind a cloud and sometimes it slipped out and hung suspended in the open sky. At this point, a milky-white light shone down on the rail tracks, like clear water flowing through willow and poplar branches. A pungent odor of gasoline surged up from the tracks and hovered over the train station, like dawn mist strolling through the morning light. When the moon emerged, the light under the platform promptly dimmed, and when the moonlight faded, the platform lamps lit up again.

The three of us stood in an empty area in the middle of the platform and gazed at one another under the light from the lamps and the moon. Then we looked at the sky, at the railroad tracks, and at several dark train cars that were slumbering in the distance. It was as if it were only then that I finally realized I was going to leave Fourth Uncle and Shucheng. I was pursuing a seemingly impossible objective. At this instant, everyone became anxious, as though they suddenly remembered they still had a lot to say and do, and if they didn't act now they might never again have the opportunity. My cousin carried my bag and walked back and forth along the train platform, as though he knew where a certain train car was going to stop and where the door would open, and therefore wanted to position himself correctly. Before the train arrived, Fourth Uncle took out a pile of bills that had been carefully folded and wrapped in paper, and stuffed them into my hand. This was a hundred yuan, which he wanted me to take back to my parents. He said I was leaving in a hurry and therefore wouldn't have time to go back to the factory to clear my account and collect my salary, and so he was giving me those hundred yuan to take to his elder brother and sister-in-law. He said that although he had been working in the factory for more than twenty years, having started before he turned twenty, he nevertheless had rarely given even a cent to his brothers. He explained that the money was a subsidy for my parents, which is to say his brother and sister-in-law. He said that at the end of the month, he would collect my entire salary, and when he went home for New Year's he would pass it on to me.

Naturally, I couldn't accept Fourth Uncle's money. Although he had a job outside, and I had previously viewed him as an urban resident, during those two years that I had been working with him I had spent approximately seven hundred days coming to appreciate his frustration and misery, his embarrassment and financial problems. During that time I had come to realize that he shouldered the miseries of both urban life and rural life, like someone suspended in midair and surrounded by thorns.

He was unable to let go—not only of the thorns but also of the red-hot steel rods on either side of him. This had been arranged by fate, so he had no choice but to continue grasping both of them for dear life.

I knew I definitely couldn't accept Fourth Uncle's money, but as we were jostling back and forth on the train platform, Fourth Uncle's eyes suddenly filled with tears, and other travelers stared at me. Shucheng said then, "Just take the money. If Fourth Uncle wants to give it to you, just take it." Shucheng then gave me a look indicating I should take it.

So I accepted the money.

Then the train arrived, as though it had been waiting for me to take the money. Before I even had a chance to stuff the packet of cash into my pocket, the train noisily stopped in front of me. No one boarded with me, but my uncle and cousin pushed me up onto the train.

As the train was leaving, I stuck my head out the window and waved to my uncle and cousin, then stuffed that neatly folded pile of bills into Fourth Uncle's hand, shouting, "Uncle . . . take this. On Sunday, I want you and Shucheng to go into the city and buy yourselves some new clothes."

In the instant Fourth Uncle took the money, I saw him standing under the lamplight and the moonlight, and noticed that his face resembled a dark yellow piece of fabric that had just been removed from a pool of water, as two tears rolled down his cheek like raindrops. After the train pulled away, my hand—which was waving in the dark—gradually fell still. Fourth Uncle and Shucheng's shadows grew increasingly small and faint until they were specks of dust.

8. RETURNING HOME

In the end, I wasn't fated to pass the university examinations.

At the end of the year, when Fourth Uncle returned home to visit his family, I bowed my head and told him I hadn't passed.

Fourth Uncle laughed and said, "Then why don't you return to the factory with me?"

I replied, "Next year I want to join the army."

In the end, I did in fact join the army.

I entered the city.

Then I was demobilized.

After I was demobilized, since I loved literature, the army summoned me back and promoted me to cadre, and I married a city girl. When I got married, I wrote Fourth Uncle a letter, and in response he offered me his congratulations, repeatedly emphasizing that I should "enjoy life." He said that life was important, but that nothing could surpass having a secure and stable existence. This was 1984—my love for literature was like my love for my wife, and my attachment to my family was like my attachment to my writing. Although I initially published several stories as mere exercises, I ended up feeling a growing desire for success and recognition. In order to publish a story in the Kaifeng journal *Dongjing Literature*, I went with a couple of fellow soldiers and took a pot of jasmine from the Shangqiu barracks greenhouse and placed it in the window of my dormitory. That weekend, I picked up that large flowerpot, which weighed several dozen *jin*, and took it into the Shangqiu train station through a side door where they didn't check tickets, then placed it in the aisle of a train. Next, I played hide-and-seek with the ticket attendant—repeatedly moving from one train car to another and periodically stepping into the bathroom to avoid the attendant. Finally, two and a half hours later, when the train stopped at the Kaifeng station, I grabbed the flowerpot and got off. I didn't leave the train station through the main entrance but rather continued forward along the train tracks until I reached a field, and from there was able to cross over into the ancient capital of Kaifeng City. I met up with my wife, and we proceeded to take that flowerpot to the office of the editor of *Dongjing Literature*.

For a long time, because of my feverish investment in my family and my literature, I didn't properly consider the questions of "living" in the countryside and "life" in the city, nor did I attempt to determine whether—after I established my own family—what I would be leading would be "living" or "life." So when Fourth Uncle wrote me a letter urging me to "enjoy life," I didn't stop to consider whether Fourth Uncle himself was enjoying a combination of living and life, or whether the two were completely separate for him. Finally, one day I went out on business, and when I returned home Fourth Uncle suddenly appeared before me, and it was only then that I realized that he was already fifty-eight and had retired. After he retired, his daughter Suping took over his job, while he returned from Xinxiang to move back into his old family house.

My fifty-eight-year-old retired fourth uncle was like a river that suddenly becomes obstructed and doubles back upon itself. I didn't dare believe that he, who had previously worked at the factory, often doing overtime, was now almost sixty. I couldn't believe that he, who once had jet-black hair, had now gone completely gray. I couldn't believe that he, who once had a clear voice and a ruddy complexion, was now pale and asthmatic. This made me realize that those of us from my generation would always need our parents' love, from our youth to middle age. As long as our parents remained healthy, we would forever treat them as though they were still in their thirties or forties, and we would forever view ourselves as immature children in need of our parents' love—even if by that point we were already adults, and the members of our parents' generation were already entering old age. Because this sort of tender love resembled a river constantly flowing out from its source, we assumed that it was inexhaustible. In fact, we would often view that love as a burden and would want to discard our elders' love the same way that someone might lance a boil on their back. Eventually the day would arrive when the older generation would grow old and fall ill, and only then would we understand how our parents and their generation had exhausted themselves for the sake of their children and for the sake of daily life and daily trifles. As for us, by that point we would no longer be children, youths, or young adults.

At the time, we neglected our parents and their generation the same way that we ravenously sucked their lifeblood as though it were water. Now, however, we remember that we are the children of our parents and the descendants of that older generation. Up to now, our parents and their generation have done everything humanly possible on our behalf. Now they are elderly and can no longer work the fields or go to work in the factories, and the only thing to keep them company is futility and aging. Now that the only thing they have to look forward to is disease and death, we should understand that our role is not just to be parents to our children or spouses to our partners. We should struggle not only on behalf of our careers and aspirations, but rather we should also apply a portion of our efforts to help our parents. We should take one of the twenty-eight bones in our fingers and let our parents use and caress it. We should let them appreciate the fact that, in this life, they did indeed give birth to and raise some children.

We should endeavor to let them enjoy the process of living as though it were life itself, and let them enjoy life as though it were completely different from living.

I recall how, when I got married, Fourth Uncle repeatedly reminded me that I should enjoy life. I recall Fourth Uncle's life, and how he vacillated between living and life, and even the embarrassment and exhaustion of his struggle. I recall how, when he finally retired, he was able to let out his breath—like a boat, continually buffeted back and forth on a river, that can find shelter by the shore, permitting the passengers to disembark and have a smoke or enjoy a leisurely drink.

Fourth Uncle liked to drink. His two sons were honest, upright, and extremely filial, and his grandchildren crowded around him every day in an adoring fashion. Every month he received a pension, because he had spent half his life as a bowed-head, living away from Fourth Aunt. After he retired, he and Fourth Aunt were able to live and enjoy their old age together, and Fourth Aunt treated Fourth Uncle very considerately. I assumed that Fourth Uncle would be able to enjoy a peaceful and happy life. When I returned I sat with him in front of our house for more than two hours, chatting about all sorts of matters, but when he finally shifted to the topic of his life, he stared blankly, then smiled wanly, and said a soft voice, "After having worked outside the village for half my life, now that I've returned home I find that I can't adjust."

He was silent for a while and then added softly, "The main thing is that I feel that I don't fit in with anyone."

At first, I didn't know how to respond, nor did I understand the significance of his remark. Instead, it was only after he left that I gradually realized that Fourth Uncle had spent his entire life as a wanderer. He resided in the gap between the city and the country-side. If the city, in the eyes of those from the countryside, was a lofty heaven, while the countryside was a form of hell on earth, his life for more than forty years had been suspended in midair. This state of being unable to reach heaven while also being unable to return to earth had become a familiar and unalterable reality for him. He was like a bird that has spent half its life in a bird cage hanging from a tree branch—if you release it, it won't be able to adjust either to flying through the sky or to walking on the ground and instead will be comfortable only suspended in between, sitting in a tree that sways in the breeze. Fourth Uncle was the same way. He belonged neither to the city nor to the countryside, and in the end he possessed a life that belonged only to him and others with his circumstances. Bowed-heads like him had their own friends and social circles, their own concerns and topics of conversation. They had their own experiences of and solutions to serious issues like life, fate, the country, and the nation, and they also had their own understandings of and replies to common matters of oil, salt, vinegar, soy sauce, and their children's romantic entanglements. They were a group of people who had left their land and, in order to seek riches in the city, had resigned themselves to a life of material hardship, spiritual turmoil, and endless deprivation. They were homesick on account of having left the countryside to go to the city, like so many generations before them, but they were also sojourners who, because of their homesickness, were unable to fully integrate into city life. Among the Chinese people, those who do not suffer from homesickness can be counted as fortunate. Those who do may find it of value for writing, but it is a burden for life. If you suffer from homesickness but do not write, it is like having a chunk of unrefined gold but not one beautifully crafted piece of jewelry.

Of course, among these homesick city dwellers, the happiest are those who have succeeded in their struggle to become officials and businesspeople. Because they were originally born in the countryside, however, their hometown becomes an endless source of bittersweet memories. If a rural resident manages to leave the countryside and achieve success, such that he acquires a retinue following his golden sedan, then when he returns to his hometown to visit his family and friends, this will almost inevitably constitute a moment of redemption.

However, Fourth Uncle was different. He led a simple life and was constantly short of money. After he worked outside for forty years, his only major achievements were raising his children and building them tile-roofed houses that quickly went out of fashion—as happened to many families who stayed behind to work the land. The only difference was that when this mode of living in the gaps between buildings became an essential part of Fourth Uncle's being, this entire way of life was suddenly cut short. As a result, there were so many things that would appear to have no direct connection to Fourth Uncle's life, but when he reached the point that he could reminisce about them, he finally understood that he did have an intricate relationship with them, and that they were part of his life, his fate, and his blood. Everything from housing, hygiene, health care, street life, transportation, shopping, his practice of getting together with other workers to chat after work, or to drink tea or wine, and even the places that seemed close but which he would never visit—the shopping malls, skyscrapers, movie theaters, white-collar businesses—to the city youths who would hurry past him and the city children constantly being shuttled to and from school by their parents. These all formed part of his spirit.

This was particularly true of the sort of soul and spirit that Fourth Uncle's lifestyle helped cultivate. This type of environment had already become something Fourth Uncle could no longer fully comprehend—he was like monks or nuns who spend their entire life in a monastery, tolling the morning and evening bells. While the monastery is still around they don't consider it their spirit or soul, and instead they feel that it is simply their home. However, if one day it suddenly collapses, disappears, or is moved—or if it remains intact but they themselves are driven away—then at that point they finally understand that the monastery, with the monotonous tolling of its bells, was not merely their home and life but also their soul and spirit.

In this case, what has moved or changed was not merely the monastery and its environment but also the person's belief and interior world.

We can't really explain how, exactly, an external "object" or "other" like the monastery can become the monk's or nun's soul and spirit, and it is quite possible that the monk or nun can't explain it either. In Buddhism it is always claimed that "Buddhism resides in the heart" and not in an "object" or "other." Without this sort of "object" or "other," however, a monk or nun cannot have a soul or spirit.

Fourth Uncle was like that monk or nun. Although no one had demolished his monastery or driven him out of the tile-roofed building where he had spent half a lifetime tolling the morning and evening bells, fate nevertheless required that he leave the city and return to that seemingly familiar hometown that had been a source of anxiety for him his entire life. Of course, only after he returned to his hometown, where he knew virtually everyone, did he finally realize that while the city did not belong to him, neither did the countryside, and even those people he thought he knew well were virtual strangers.

Fourth Uncle experienced profound solitude and loneliness.

Day after day, he experienced a sense of spiritual weakness and loss.

Today, we understand that behind the bustling life in the countryside, there is in fact a deep stillness. Peasants no longer work the land and have to travel long distances to find employment. Every family's fields lie fallow, and even during the busy agricultural season there is only a handful of children and old people out working. In daily life, the young people who don't go looking for employment in the cities stay in the village to work in chicken farms and pig farms, where they also live. And so the village comes to resemble a battle-ground after an army has passed through, and even the brand-new houses and bridal chambers cannot conceal the village's decline and its resulting stillness.

When a village loses its liveliness, it also loses its soul.

After a village loses its soul, it will never again regain its former liveliness.

After Fourth Uncle retired and returned home, he kept watch over the houses, streets, villages, and over the stillness itself, like an old man guarding a cemetery in the wilderness. Those children and elders who remained behind in the village "never had anything to say" to him, the same way that he didn't share any interests with them. The villagers didn't know what Fourth Uncle really cared about, and although Fourth Uncle did know what *they* cared about, he didn't share those concerns. His daughter inherited his position in the Xinxiang cement factory, while his second son and daughter-in-law also went to work in the factory, just as I had done. Fourth Uncle's eldest son and his family remained behind in the village, but every day they, like everyone else, had to keep busy raising pigs and pursuing various small ventures just in order to survive. Regardless of how filial they might be, they would never be able to counteract Fourth Uncle's sense of loss and loneliness, and even less would they be able to change Fourth Uncle's spirit, that of a monk who has lost his monastery. In order to alleviate Fourth Uncle's sense of loss, his eldest son, Changke, not only made a point of speaking to him regularly but also encouraged him to enjoy himself by playing mahjong.

Changke always hoped that his father would be able to return from the city and reintegrate with his original rural life, even if others might find that life boring.

Changke did everything he could to fulfill his duties as a filial son.

Several times, I told him, "Fourth Uncle likes to drink. So if he wants, you should let him drink some every day. Just make sure he doesn't drink too much."

Changke replied, "I let him drink some every day. I know that drinking helps relieve some of his boredom."

I added, "If he wants to play mahjong, then let him play with some of the other villagers. Just make sure that he doesn't play for money."

Changke said, "I'm afraid he'll develop a habit."

In this way, after Fourth Uncle retired, he entered a state of boredom and would spend the entire day standing around and looking at nothing. The village streets were empty, and often he'd be the only person there, standing in the village entrance like a useless tree. Over time, he interacted more and more with his wine cups and bottles, sharing with them all of his life experiences and fated arrangements. Later, when he didn't have anything else to do, he'd seat himself at the village mahjong table. Because he received a pension, idlers were eager to play with him, and sometimes several of them would join together and invite him to play as soon as he received his monthly stipend, encouraging him to gamble it all away. In this way, they used mahjong to transfer his pension into their own pockets.

9. RETURN

In his old age, Fourth Uncle would frequently be kept company by his wine cup or mahjong table. At first, each time I returned, I would always bring him a bottle or two, but later Mother told me to stop. She explained that when Fourth Uncle drank, he would lose his senses. He would go looking for people to play mahjong with, but his gambling partners would often cheat him, and although this was obvious to everyone, Fourth Uncle himself remained oblivious.

When I mentioned to Changke that Fourth Uncle seemed to have developed a gambling problem and a drinking problem, his eyes became bloodshot, and he replied that he didn't know why his father had turned out this way. Changke said that if they didn't let his father drink and gamble, he found life very boring, but if they let him enjoy himself, he would ignore even his own family.

Changke said regretfully, "If we had realized this sooner, we would never have helped him find mahjong partners." However, I could tell that Changke understood the source of his father's feelings of loss and loneliness. The other people who had gone back to the village after having worked in the city ended up returning to the city upon realizing that they couldn't reacclimate to life in the countryside. Because of this, the village is no longer what it once was. Those who come back from the city might appear to be the same people they were when they left the countryside, but in reality they aren't. They are like a pair of shattered mirrors. Even if after several decades you finally succeed in piecing the fragments back together, the mirrors will never again be truly complete. Because of differences in collection and preservation, the color and brightness of the various fragments will have corroded to differing degrees. However, Fourth Uncle didn't have the option of returning to the city—both because Fourth Aunt wasn't willing and also because his pension from the cement factory was not very large, and it couldn't begin to approach his previous monthly salary. My cousins Suping and Jianke led a very difficult life and frequently had to work overtime in the cement factory. Compared to them, Changke, who was living at home, was comparatively well-off, thanks to his diligence and industriousness.

Therefore, Fourth Uncle had no choice but to remain in his family home.

It seemed that Fourth Uncle had no choice but to use alcohol and gambling to compensate for his sense of loss and loneliness. Finally, in 2007, on National Day—which is to say, on the twenty-first day of the eighth month on the lunar calendar—my mother suddenly called me up long-distance and told me to come home as soon as possible, because Fourth Uncle had just passed away. She said that he had been gambling and drinking again and, after getting drunk, had fallen into a gully and badly injured himself. Although he was taken to the hospital, he still departed this world two days later. Next, my elder brother phoned me and urged me to hurry home, after which my eldest sister did the same. I quickly packed my bags and bought a train ticket, but I couldn't make it home until the next day. Once there, just as I had done two years earlier, following First Uncle's death, I proceeded to keep vigil by Fourth Uncle's spirit tent, staying beside his coffin and his corpse, which would never again take a breath in this mortal world. I kept vigil until we sent Fourth Uncle to his grave plot, where he could lie with his two elder brothers, my father and first uncle. Before I returned again to Beijing, I went to see my cousin Changke, whose eyes were bloodshot and whose knees were bloody from kowtowing. When Changke and his wife saw me, they were silent for a long time, until finally Changke broke the silence and said, "If only my father could have remained in the city after he retired, rather than going home to the countryside." Changke observed that his father's relocation to the countryside from the city precipitated a change not only in his father's process of daily living but also in his life and his fate.

As Changke was saying this, his tear-filled eyes dried up. He appeared calm and thoughtful, as though he had already fully experienced the city and the countryside, life and fate, marriage and love, life and daily life—these sorts of matters that peasants often do not actively consider, despite the fact that they are often immersed within them. It is as though they have already made preparation for the future and for life's magical transformation.

10. INSIDE AND OUTSIDE THE WALL

By this point, all three brothers from Father's generation have left us. They've all left this life's disorder and confusion and have bid farewell to this world's happiness and misery. In my family, there was a saying: "If members of the elder generation were any older, they'd be a tree shielding us from the wind." What this meant was that regardless of how old or sick the elders might be, as long as they are still alive, you will feel that you yourself are young. As long as nothing unexpected happens and death arrives when expected, the elderly resemble a tree planted in front of a forest, blocking the specter of death from entering the forest and preventing it from interacting with others. Similarly, the elderly use their old age and their feeble bodies to keep death outside, where they can then engage it in a discussion, a debate, or a struggle. If they can force death to admit defeat, then death will end up passing by our family, our front door, and our forest. Otherwise, if death is able to outtalk the elderly, they will have no choice but to depart together with death, in order to prevent it from bothering those of us in the next generation. Alternatively, if death starts heading toward one's family and one's plot of forest like a whirlwind, the elders will resist and struggle. Finally, when they are completely exhausted, they will use their final ounce of strength to lead death away from the family's doorstep and the edge of its forest, and then they will depart together with death.

The condition under which death leaves the forest or the family's courtyard is that our elders will not be permitted to return. The elders have no choice but to accept this condition, and because they are already elderly, they have no ground on which to negotiate. If they don't take a first step, it's possible that death may enter the forest and topple another tree, or enter a family's courtyard and bother someone else.

The elderly have no choice but to take a first step on behalf of the next generation. Then they go to the next world and lie down there, calmly waiting for their children to follow in their footsteps and be reunited with them. My father left us twenty-five years ago. First Uncle left three years ago—and the twenty-sixth day of the first month of the next lunar year will mark the third anniversary of his death. Meanwhile, it has already been more than a year since Fourth Uncle left us. As everyone else was joining in the National Day celebrations three months ago, our family was observing the anniversary of his death. When I think back on it, it occurs to me that Father's premature demise was in order to prevent death from crossing the threshold of our house and finding his wife and children, which is why he was always standing guard in the entranceway to our courtyard, or at the edge of the forest, using his sickly body to protect our lives—until ultimately he had no choice but to leave us and lead death away. As for First Uncle, he had spent his entire life resisting fate and struggling for survival, until he stopped struggling with fate and instead spent ten years struggling with death. Before he finally left us, I think First Uncle assumed he had succeeded in defeating death, as a result of which death offered him a compromise: it seemed that death decided to leave out of respect for his fortitude and perseverance, and therefore First Uncle relaxed, assuming that because he could no longer see death, it meant it had truly departed and wouldn't pay any attention to his family in the immediate future. Eventually, however, death rushed up to First Uncle, catching him and our family by surprise.

First Uncle was ultimately killed by his inaction and carelessness in the face of death.

As for Fourth Uncle, he does not appear to have had many theories about or arguments with death, but then again, neither did he have many struggles with death, as First Uncle did. In his bones,

Fourth Uncle was like me, too weak and quiet. He was constantly thinking about things but wasn't willing to discuss them, and he was willing to do things but wasn't willing to debate them. Sometimes he didn't think because he was too busy doing. When he didn't have anything to do, he would silently reflect, and if he still couldn't figure things out after thinking for a long time, he would abandon himself to drink and gambling. Although Fourth Uncle liked to drink, he wasn't a drunkard; and although he liked to gamble, he wasn't a problem gambler. He used alcohol and gambling for socializing, sustenance, and distraction. Like a tree, he entrusted his life to the cracks between rocks and sand. If there was a normal amount of sun and rain, the tree would grow vigorously, but if there was a sudden wind, it wouldn't be able to resist and would end up getting blown over.

Compared to the lives of Father and First Uncle, Fourth Uncle's life appeared relatively fragile, because he was perennially plagued by problems we didn't know about, and which he ultimately wasn't able to resolve. Father, meanwhile, departed early, and his affections were smooth and soothing, and he was loving and kind toward daily life, his children, and life in general. However, in the end, he had no choice but to leave this world for the sake of our survival. First Uncle lived to the age of eighty-two, and although he departed abruptly and undeservedly, when we later remembered him, he always renewed our respect and reverence for life.

In the end, Father, First Uncle, and Fourth Uncle all departed. Father's death marked the first opening in the protective wall surrounding our family, and when the wind subsequently blew through this opening, it prematurely toppled the life trees of two children, my cousins Tiecheng and Lianyun. Over the past three years, following the departures of First Uncle and Fourth Uncle, a section of the protective wall around our family has not only been breached but completely collapsed. Third Uncle and his wife, Third Aunt, are still alive, but they are already in their seventies, and their life is not easy. First Aunt, Mother, and Fourth Aunt are in their late seventies or eighties, and furthermore First Aunt and Fourth Aunt are ill, and their thinking and speech are no longer very clear.

Mother, meanwhile, is in relatively good health, and while she takes medicine every day, her mind nevertheless is still as sharp as when she was young. If you view our family from a practical perspective, the fortunate thing about my father's generation and First Aunt, Mother, Third Aunt, and Fourth Aunt is that they are all blessed with very filial children. Between one generation and the next, there are some who are so filial that they could be compared to traditional models of family piety, and although in contemporary society the word *filiality* might appear old and shallow, in the countryside it still represents life's greatest comfort and dignity. The fortunate thing for those of us in the younger generations is that Third Uncle, Third Aunt, First Aunt, Fourth Aunt, and my mother are still alive, so even though one section of the barrier wall protecting our clan may have toppled, others are still standing and sufficient to prevent that dark wind from recklessly blowing in.

In the end, however, it remains true that an entire section of that wall is now missing, and if we gaze out through that opening, we clearly see death and the notice it is carrying, and we can clearly hear its footsteps approaching and its low voice on the road. So we have no choice but to consider the answer and remuneration we will offer, just as we have no choice but to consider the attitude with which we will subsequently face our own death and fate, together with how we will respond to, argue with, and struggle against death. Life must always come to an end, and that final day will inevitably come, so it is necessary to consider those who will live on.

Translator's Note

Issues of language and kinship are at the heart of Yan Lianke's *Three Brothers*. In many respects, kinship terminology is much more granular in Chinese than in English. For instance, there is no single term in Chinese for male sibling that would be equivalent to the English word *brother*. Instead, there are different Chinese terms depending on whether the individual in question is older or younger than the speaker (e.g., *gege* for "elder brother" and *didi* for "younger brother"), and furthermore, it is also common to specify the siblings' ages relative *to one another* (e.g., *dage*, *erge*, and *sange*, to refer to someone's eldest brother, second elder brother, and third elder brother, respectively). A similar point can be made with respect to the siblings from one's parents' generation: where English, for instance, uses a single term (*uncle*) to refer to all of a mother's or father's male siblings, in Chinese there are different terms depending on whether the individual in question is one of the father's elder brothers, one of his younger brothers, one of the mother's elder brothers, or one of her younger brothers. In addition to this fourfold differentiation, it is also common to specify the uncles' ages relative *to one another* (e.g., *dabo*, *erbo*, and *sanbo*, to refer to the father's eldest brother, second elder brother, and third elder brother, respectively).

At the same time, however, there are also other respects in which Chinese tends to *elide* kinship distinctions that are usually specified in English. For instance, it is common for Chinese to consider multiple different generations as belonging to the same large family (such as in the traditional ideal of *wudai tongtang*, or "five generations under one roof"), and consequently it is common to refer to extended relatives as though they were closer than they actually are. For instance, Yan Lianke's memoir technically distinguishes between the author's immediate siblings and his cousins, but at various points the male cousins are instead referred to simply as *gege* or *didi* (literally, "elder brother" and "younger brother"). Similarly, the original Chinese title of the work, which could be translated literally as *Me and My Father's Generation*, refers to the author's father and three other men from his generation—and of these three other men, two are the father's brothers, while the third is actually the father's (paternal-side) cousin. In English, we would call the first two men "uncles" and would call the third something else (technically, he would be "first cousin once removed"). In Chinese, however, the relevant terminological distinction is not between the father's brother and his cousin (the narrator refers to both of them as *shu*), but rather it is between the uncle who is older than the father (and whom the narrator refers to as *dabo* [literally, "eldest uncle on the father's side"]), and the two "uncles" who are younger than the father (*sanshu* and *sishu* [literally, "third eldest younger uncle on the father's side" and "fourth eldest younger uncle on the father's side"]).

In translating *Three Brothers*, I have approached these various terminological challenges in slightly different ways. On one hand, I've followed the Chinese convention of embedding a reference to birth order into terms for siblings, uncles, aunts, and so forth, although one would rarely do so in English. On the other hand, where the volume refers affectionately to the author's cousins as "brothers," in my translation I have instead followed the English-language convention and referred to them as "cousins" (to help prevent unnecessary confusion). Apart from this particular adjustment, however, I have generally refrained from adjusting or parsing culturally or historically specific terminology.

The memoir does include numerous parenthetical remarks that add useful contextual information—for instance, when an ill-informed teacher avers that Henan University might be in the provincial capital of Zhengzhou, this is followed by a parenthetical note specifying that, "In fact, it's in Kaifeng." In this and every other instance, these parenthetical notes have not been added to the manuscript for the benefit of English-language readers, but rather they were already present in the original Chinese text.